MW00436874

Queen
of the Home

OTHER BOOKS *from* VISION FORUM

Queen of the Home

Essays, Poetry, and Quotes on the
Honor, Nobility, and Power of Biblical Womanhood

Compiled and Edited by Jennifer M. McBride

THE VISION FORUM, INC.
SAN ANTONIO, TEXAS

First Printing
Copyright © 2011 The Vision Forum, Inc.
All Rights Reserved

"Where there is no vision, the people perish." (Proverbs 29:18)

The Vision Forum, Inc.
4719 Blanco Rd., San Antonio, Texas 78212
www.visionforum.com

ISBN 978-1-434554-60-9

Cover Design and Typography by Justin Turley

Printed in the United States of America

To My Daughters

Catherine Marie, Isabelle Grace,
Emma Jane, and Priscilla Mercy

May each of you know, love, and serve the
King of Kings with all your heart, soul, and mind.

May you grow from beautiful girlhood into
godly, noble womanhood and reign someday
as happy queens in homes of your own.

Table of Contents

Acknowledgments

My deep appreciation to the men and women who graciously contributed to this book:

Nancy Campbell
www.aboverubies.org

Karen Andreola
www.homeschoolhighlights.com

Rebecca Morecraft
www.chalcedon.org

Stacy McDonald
www.yoursacredcalling.com
www.passionatehousewives.com

Jennie Chancey
www.ladiesagainstfeminism.com
www.sensibility.com

Anna Sofia and Elizabeth Botkin
www.visionarydaughters.com

June Fuentes
www.proverbs14verse1.blogspot.com

Rebecca Serven Loomis
www.genevanfoundation.com
www.reflecthymn.com

Elizabeth Serven Ten Dolle

Doug and Beall Phillips
www.visionforum.com

Kelly Crawford
www.generationcedar.com

Crystal Paine
www.moneysavingmom.com

Craig and Barbara Smith
www.hef.org.nz

My thanks also to:

My faithful Lord and Saviour, Jesus Christ, who saw fit to save me and Who continues to draw me into an ever deeper knowledge of Himself and the beautiful truths of His Holy Word.

My beloved husband Steve: You are my knight in shining armor and the king of our castle. Thank you for the godly way you rule our home, for your persevering spirit, loving me far more than I deserve and for treating me like a queen. It is an honor to be your wife, and I thank the Lord for you. I love you more than I can say.

My eight precious children, Catherine, William, Isabelle, Emma, Samuel, Gideon, Mercy, and our little baby on the way. Each one of you is a special gift straight from the Hand of Almighty God. Through your young lives the Lord is teaching me many important lessons. Thank you for trusting love, hugs, kisses and cards made just for me. Truly you are a "reward"(Psalm 127).

My parents for setting my feet on the old paths even when the way was lonely and people thought you were crazy. May the sacrifices you made then bear much eternal fruit.

All my brothers and sisters (including those by marriage) for godly encouragement, the immense amount of practical help that you have given to me, being wonderful aunties and uncles to my children and most of all, your close friendships. You and yours are so dear to me and mine.

Grandpa and Nanna for your example of a long and faithful marriage, and for your prayers, packages, cards, and long-distance encouragement. I so wish we could live closer and sit down for a cup of tea, some Welsh cakes, and a good long visit.

Jennie Chancey for being a godly mentor, example, inspiration, and long-distance kindred spirit. It is through you that the Lord first led me into a richer understanding of the incredible power of Biblical womanhood.

Foreword

The volume you hold in your hands is a treasure trove. You are about to dive into centuries of wisdom and encouragement that will challenge you, renew your vision, and refresh your spirit. My friend Jennifer McBride has done a great service in pulling together resources to inspire Christian women in their calling as keepers at home.

Sadly, you will find little of this encouragement in the broader culture, particularly in the West. Having rejected our Lawgiver, it seems we are now determined to blot out even the faintest memory of the good, noble, and true path He graciously gave us to walk. All around us, voices cry out that we are "worth it," that we are powerful, capable, and strong . . . as long as we turn our backs on "quaint" notions like homekeeping, rearing our own children, preparing meals, demonstrating hospitality on a regular basis, and showing respect and honor to our husbands. It seems in today's world, a woman can be fulfilled in any way . . . as long as that way doesn't involve her own home or family.

At the same time, we are bombarded with the utterly false idea that women can "have it all"—the happy marriage, motherhood, and full-time career—all at the same time. But none of us can do this. We simply cannot be in two places at once, concentrating our full attention on the demands of a career while also giving our all to husbands, children, home, and church. Common sense should confirm this, but we seem to have rejected common sense along with God's perfect will for families. Instead of ruling in our own sphere, we have become slaves in another's. The loss to our civilization has been devastating, for without home-building wives and mothers, culture disintegrates.

Queen of the Home reminds us of our birthright as women, and it is a rich and beautiful one. In the beginning, God set Adam and Eve as king and queen over creation. They were designed to complement one another. It wasn't good for man to be alone, as God Himself stated. Man needed woman to complete him as his perfect helper. Without woman, godly dominion simply could not take place. With his helper, Adam could tend and keep the garden, drawing on Eve's gifts and abilities, and be fruitful as God commanded. The Fall harmed that perfect union and distorted the mysterious and holy marriage relationship, but Christ's finished work on the cross redeems us from the Fall and calls us back to co-laboring as husbands and wives, each with important roles to fulfill as we serve the Lord. In turn, our laboring together in harmony presents a picture of Christ and His bride, the Church. What a glorious calling!

Jennifer McBride has given us a powerful dose of inspiration and vision in this volume. I am thankful for her willingness to put it together, and I look forward to sharing it with family and friends. I pray you will be blessed as you enjoy these pages and meditate on the importance of the amazing, multi-faceted role God has given you. You are queen of your home! May your home reflect the glory and goodness of the God Who placed you there.

Jennie Chancey
At home,
May 2011

Introduction

Who can find a virtuous woman? for her price is far above rubies. (Proverbs 31:10)

As we look back just a few generations ago, we see a vastly different view of the keeper at home than the one commonly held today. It was a view that upheld the Biblical standard and understood that this was no mere job but a noble and sacred calling, a position of power and influence like no other.

The role of wife and mother was held in high esteem in the past, and considered worthy of great honor, appreciation, and respect. The homemaker was seen as strong, capable, intelligent and irreplaceable, not only a crucial part of the home, but a foundational bulwark of society.

Sadly, much has changed. Over the last century Biblical womanhood has been under extreme fire from radical feminists and Marxists. In their attempts to annihilate the traditional, God-ordained family unit, they have rightly understood that one of their top strategies must be not only to attack and destroy strong manhood, but to remove women from their rightful sphere.

One of their most successful tactics has been to belittle and demean the role of the woman at home, passionately proclaiming that this is a worse-than-useless position and one to be eschewed at all costs. Those whom they fail to convince to actually leave their homes are made to feel as though they are wasting their lives in mindless drudgery and that they are even a drain on society.

Consider this small sampling of quotes from prominent feminists and humanists:

> *The chief thing is to get women to take part in socially productive labor, to liberate them from 'domestic slavery,' to free them from their stupefying and humiliating subjugation to the eternal drudgery of the kitchen and the nursery. This struggle will be a long one, and it demands a radical reconstruction, both of social technique and of morale. But it will end in the complete triumph of Communism.*

—V.I. Lenin, *International Working Women's Day Speech* , 1920

[The] housewife is a nobody, and [housework] is a dead-end job. It may actually have a deteriorating effect on her mind . . . rendering her incapable of prolonged concentration on any single task. [She] comes to seem dumb as well as dull. [B]eing a housewife makes women sick.

—Sociologist Jessie Bernard,
The Future of Marriage, 1982

A parasite sucking out the living strength of another organism . . . the [housewife's] labor does not even tend toward the creation of anything durable. . . . [W]oman's work within the home [is] not directly useful to society, produces nothing. [The housewife] is subordinate, secondary, parasitic. It is for their common welfare that the situation must be altered by prohibiting marriage as a 'career for woman.'

—Simone de Beauvoir,
The Second Sex, 1949

Tragically, multitudes of women have drunk deeply at feminism's well—often without quite realizing just what it was they were imbibing. Though at times it is diluted and administered in more palatable forms then the shocking statements above, the poison of this radical, anti-God, anti-family movement has permeated the thinking of the entire world—including Christendom— and the consequences have been devastating.

The role of the keeper at home, once deeply appreciated and honored, is now looked upon as an insult to the intelligence of today's woman. The woman who actually wants to be home with her family is made to feel foolish and guilty. Any one can do laundry, change diapers, make a meal and wipe noses, right, so why not hire someone else to handle these chores? Why should modern women waste their time and ambitions on such things when they can go out and unleash their talents on the world?

As a result of this insidious viewpoint, society has been turned upside down, divorce runs rampant, and children are commonly raised by daycare workers, government school teacher,s and television. Men are increasingly abandoning their roles as providers and protectors, and women are being driven to exhaustion by the myth of a super-woman who successfully juggles a husband, career, children, and time for herself.

In short, and in a terrible irony, women have willingly abdicated their God-ordained positions of honor, nobility, and strength for the lie that their true worth and destiny are found in careers outside the home.

Doug Phillips sums it up so well:

Off to war went the daughters.
Left behind the men and babes.
Noble womanhood was slaughtered
Craving freedom became slaves. [1]

Or as Stacy McDonald states in *Passionate Housewives, Desperate for God*: "Rather than women renouncing this affront to their dignity, amazingly the slaves are demanding their slavery!"

Scripture declares the truth: It is through the saving work of Christ and in a life lived according to the standard set forth in God's Holy Word that a woman is most honored and elevated to a position like no other on earth. She is given great respect, mighty responsibilities, and a specific realm over which she is to reign.

When we take a closer look at the Scriptures, what we find is quite intriguing and illuminating:

> *I will therefore that the younger women marry, bear children, guide the house, give none occasion to the adversary to speak reproachfully. (I Timothy 5:14)*

The original Greek word used for "guide the house" here is *oikodespoteō* which is translated "ruler" or "master" (This does not mean that we rule over our husbands, but it does mean that we rule with them.)

> *To be discreet, chaste, keepers at home, good, obedient to their own husbands, that the word of God be not blasphemed. (Titus 2:5)*

Here the Greek word used for "keepers at home" is *oikourgos*, which not only means to care for the home, but to guard it.

In the famous chapter of Proverbs 31, we have a detailed description that shows just how strong, capable, and influential the virtuous woman of God really is. What might not be as well known is what is packed into the actual meaning of the word "virtuous" which appears in Scripture four times:

> *And now, my daughter, fear not; I will do to thee all that thou requirest: for all the city of my people doth know that thou art a virtuous woman. (Ruth 3:11)*

> *A virtuous woman is a crown to her husband. . . . (Proverbs 12:4)*

> *Who can find a virtuous woman? For her price is far above rubies. (Proverbs 31:10)*

> *Many daughters have done virtuously, but thou excellest them all. (Proverbs 31:29)*

I used to think that the word "virtuous" as used in these texts meant "moral" or "pure." While the word "virtue" is at times translated this way, and while this meaning too should define a godly woman, this is not the meaning of the word used in the passages above. I was amazed to discover that in the original Hebrew this word is "chayil", which is also translated throughout the Bible as "strength", "ability", "valiant", "army", "host", "forces", "riches", "wealth", "substance", "power" and even "war"! No wonder such a woman is far more valuable than rubies.

The godly wife and mother is no household drudge, weak doormat, or mindless parasite. She is a mighty warrior queen who fights righteous battles at her husband's side and reigns with him over the home and domain God has given them as they work together for Christ's eternal Kingdom and glory.

What does this really mean, though, lived out in the day to day? Are these just flowery, meaningless ideals or trite platitudes? How is one supposed to go about being a Queen exactly? Is this a silly grown-up version of playing princess? Does this mean we're supposed to sweep through pristine palaces in velvet robes and tiaras—or through spotless, perfectly decorated houses in high heels, pearls, and perfectly groomed hair? Is this about doling out commands and having our every whim fulfilled? Is it about being decorative, delicate ornaments? While beauty and aesthetics certainly have their place, Biblical womanhood is not about furthering and promoting ourselves at all—it is about obeying the Word of God and dying to self. It is about advancing Christ's Kingdom. It is about the purpose for which we were created: glorifying the Almighty God.

It is one of Scripture's beautiful mysteries that in dying, we live. It is not easy. It is hard work in fact, and it involves sacrifice. This is what our Saviour modeled and what the Lord abundantly blesses. It is in the daily laying down of our lives in service to the Lord and our families—loving and helping our husbands, teaching and training our children, caring for our homes and reaching out the hand of hospitality that we are able to do a mighty work for Him. In dying to ourselves, we bear greater fruit.

> *Verily, verily, I say unto you, Except a corn of wheat fall into the ground and die, it abideth alone: but if it die, it bringeth forth much fruit. (John 12:24)*

During World War II, the bloodiest battle in the history of the United States Marines was fought on the island of Iwo Jima. Six thousand eight hundred men lost their lives in a battle that waged for thirty-six days. Inscribed outside of the military cemetery are these words:

> *When you go home*
> *Tell them for us and say*
> *For your tomorrow*
> *We gave our today.*

The soldiers of Iwo Jima laid down their lives in sacrifice to our country, and we reap the blessings of their sacrifice today. We too are in a battle as we seek to raise up armies in Christ's eternal Kingdom, and we must be willing to lay down our lives for Him. We must gladly give our todays in service to our King for the tomorrows of our children and future generations.

In the eyes of our self-centered culture, it would appear that in pursuing our rightful calling as women we are wasting our lives, but what the world views as waste,

God views as precious. The following account from Mark's Gospel illustrates this:

> *And being in Bethany in the house of Simon the leper, as he sat at meat, there came a woman having an alabaster box of ointment of spikenard very precious; and she brake the box, and poured it on his head. And there were some that had indignation within themselves, and said, Why was this waste of the ointment made? For it might have been sold for more than three hundred pence, and have been given to the poor. And they murmured against her. And Jesus said, Let her alone; why trouble ye her? she hath wrought a good work on me. For ye have the poor with you always, and whensoever ye will ye may do them good: but me ye have not always. She hath done what she could: she is come aforehand to anoint my body to the burying. Verily I say unto you, Wheresoever this gospel shall be preached throughout the whole world, this also that she hath done shall be spoken of for a memorial of her. (Mark 14:3-9)*

To some looking on, this seemed utter foolishness; spikenard was worth one year's wages. In their reasoning it made much better sense to sell it and give the proceeds to the poor; but as we see so powerfully in this story "the wisdom of this world is foolishness with God" (I Corinthians 3:19).

There is another beautiful lesson here too: Though Mary was the one to make the offering, everyone around her was blessed:

Then took Mary a pound of ointment of spikenard, very costly, and anointed the feet of Jesus, and wiped his feet with her hair: and the house was filled with the odour of the ointment. (John 12:3)

Just as the sweetsmelling savour of Mary's sacrifice filled the whole house in Bethany, our homes—and the broken, hurting culture surrounding us—will also be permeated with a beautiful fragrance when we pour out every drop of ourselves at our Saviour's feet.

As "servant queens" we must never forget the example set before us nor the great and awe-inspiring privilege we have. As we faithfully give our lives in self-sacrifice we are directly serving the Great King of Kings:

Then shall the righteous answer him, saying, Lord, when saw we thee an hungered, and fed thee? or thirsty, and gave thee drink? When saw we thee a stranger, and took thee in? or naked, and clothed thee? Or when saw we thee sick, or in prison, and came unto thee? And the King shall answer and say unto them, Verily I say unto you, Inasmuch as ye have done it unto one of the least of these my brethren, ye have done it unto me. (Matthew 25:37-40)

Much is required of us. Our days are filled with many tasks that can sometimes seem mundane and of little worth, but if we can grasp the incredible truth of what sacrificial service really means, then our entire outlook will be transformed. When done for the Lord, the commonplace will become noble, the prosaic will become beautiful, and the unimportant will become valuable.

While multitudes of Christian women are rediscovering the beauty of God's plan for womanhood and realizing the danger of abandoning their realm, the spirit of feminism can still influence our thinking if we are not on guard. Under the constant attack of our humanistic culture, we can lose our vision and forget the value and worth of our position, becoming self-absorbed, miserable, and discontent. *We can abdicate our thrones and never leave the palace.* The Deceiver would have us in just such a condition; one that would render us weak, hopeless and ineffective. For "where there is no vision, the people perish" (Proverbs 29:18).

It is imperative that we plug our ears to the lies bombarding us and to fill our hearts, souls, and minds with the unchanging truth of God's Holy Word. It is the Light that illuminates our way; it is the Two-Edged Sword with which we fight our battles; and it is the firm Foundation on which we build the little kingdoms entrusted to us. We must keep the Lord's Standard ever before us as we "Press toward the mark for the prize of the high calling of God in Christ Jesus" (Philippians 3:14).

Over the past several years, the Lord has graciously brought to my attention this collection of essays, poetry, and quotes—all clearly and strongly proclaiming the nobility, honor, and power of Biblical womanhood. It is my prayer and hope that the writings contained in this volume will renew your vision, refresh your soul, and encourage and inspire you as much as they have me.

Although Feminism continues her barrage against Biblical womanhood, we must refuse to heed her lies anymore. Let us victoriously reclaim our thrones for the sake of our families, the advancement of Christ's Kingdom, and the glory of God.

Jennifer M. McBride
May 2011

Queen
of the Home

CHAPTER ONE

Noble Womanhood

In the hands of noble womanhood, we can yet see— rising from the ashes of a broken culture—the glories of hearth and home, so that future generations will arise and declare its virtues once again.

—*Beall Phillips,* Verses of Virtue

In every ideal home there exists an essence that diffuses its fragrance—the fine flower of noble womanhood, without which the house is a habitation, not a home. Alone under the ministering care of woman may the routine of daily life be relieved and varied and the course of the household made to flow free from friction. Caressed by her gentle touch, order ranges itself, beauty finds a dwelling place, and peace enters as an abiding guest. Preeminently it is woman that idealizes the home, and with her sweet refining presence, creates its atmosphere of serenity and content.

—George H. Ellwanger

As for myself, I do not hesitate to avow that although the women of the United States are confined within the narrow circle of domestic life, and their situation is in some respects one of extreme dependence, I have nowhere seen woman occupying a loftier position; and if I were asked, now that I am drawing to the close of this work, in which I have spoken of so many important things done by the Americans, to what the singular prosperity and growing strength of that people ought mainly to be attributed, I should reply: To the superiority of their women.

—Alexis de Tocqueville, Democracy in America

Are You a Queen?
by Jennie Chancey

God Made Women to Be Queens

Have you ever heard someone say, "If I ruled the world, things would be different!"? How about, "The hand that rocks the cradle rules the world?" Did you know this saying is literally true? The ones who teach the next generation are the ones who decide who will rule the world and how it will be governed. Who rocks the cradle in our culture today? Public schools, government caretakers, strangers. . . . There are very few women left who understand the extreme importance of their role as wives and mothers—and as daughters or grandmothers.

Did you know that God gave women a special role as coheirs of grace to help take dominion of the earth, to rule it, to bring up godly children, and to help make His kingdom beautiful? Let's turn to Genesis 1:26-28: "Then God said, 'Let Us make man in Our image, according to Our likeness; let them have dominion over the fish of the sea, over the birds of the air, and over the cattle, over all the earth and over every creeping thing that creeps on the earth.' So God created man in His own image; in the image of God He created him; male and female He created them. Then God blessed them, and God said to them, 'Be fruitful and multiply; fill the earth and subdue it; have dominion over the fish of the sea, over the birds of the air, and over every living thing that moves on the earth.'"

As you see, God made man and woman together—mankind—to rule the earth and take dominion. Mankind is male and female together; each one with a different and beautiful role. And each role complements the other and helps the other.

The Ideal Woman of Scripture Was Described by a Woman

Feminists today like to dismiss the Bible as "just a bunch of rules made up by men to keep women oppressed." But do you know who gave us the picture of the ideal woman? King Lemuel's mother did! Look at Proverbs 31:1: "The words of King Lemuel, the utterance which his mother taught him." It is mothers who are to teach their sons— not just their daughters—what kind of woman makes the ideal wife and helpmate.

We all know about that wonderful Proverbs 31 woman. She manages an entire household, ordering exotic foods, planting vineyards, commanding servants, creating beautiful clothing for herself and her children, teaching with kindness and wisdom, demonstrating godly ability in her special role. But the entire Bible is filled with women we can admire and model ourselves upon. Think of Sarah, who willingly accompanied her husband on a long journey to a strange land, calling him "lord" . . . even when he made some foolish decisions! Think of Abigail, who quickly pacified King David with her hospitality and humility after her husband, Nabal, had insulted the king and his men. Think of Esther, who risked her life to save her people by spreading a feast for her husband and his chief adviser, showing her ability to work within the king's laws even when she needed to ask for something that would break a new law he had just passed. And there are countless others, including John the Baptist's mother Elizabeth; Mary, who humbly declared to the angel, "Be it unto me according to your word" (Luke 1:38) when she was told she would give birth to Christ; the women who provided Jesus with food and shelter; Lydia, who let the church meet in her own household.

What ties all of the great women of Scripture together? Some were beautiful; some were not. Some had opportunities to do something amazing; others simply did what was right at hand in their own families. What they all share is a common bond of obedience to God's Word, joyful submission to their special role, and a willingness to be used of God in the way God designed for them.

What is Our Role at Home?

So what's so great about being at home? How could serving at home possibly be important in the grand scheme of things? After all, isn't staying at home just about doing dishes, cleaning floors, and wiping runny noses? What's so important about all that? Friends, this is exactly what Satan would like us to think about the woman's role in the home. He is delighted when the home is reduced to a list of chores. The feminists of the 1960s called homemakers "parasites," "drudges," and "mindless drones." Those are actual quotes! Is the woman at home a drain on society? A mindless parasite who just slumps along from one menial task to the next? If this is your idea of homemaking, it's time to change your vision. God's vision of the keeper at home is so beautiful, so all-encompassing, and so vital to the health of our world that it cannot be reduced to lists of chores. Let's look at what the home is about.

First of all, the home is a tiny world—a cosmos all to itself. Do you want to rule the world? God has given you the entire universe of your home to manage and "subdue." You as the "despot" of the house (this is the original Greek word for "keeper at home") are in truth the ruler of this domain. You are the queen. Your job is to make your kingdom a small picture of God's greater kingdom—a kingdom in which the subjects are in order and obey their king; a kingdom where beauty shines in every word and deed; a kingdom that welcomes friends and strangers with abundant hospitality and gracious care. Do you find our current culture disgusting and revolting? Look around at the homes that make up our culture. There is the root of the problem. Homes that are emptied of their meaning and purpose create the culture in which we live. When homes do not have creative, happy, intelligent mothers, their occupants go elsewhere to learn how to behave, to learn what music to love, to learn what art to imitate. Are you building culture in your home? Are you training your children to be the image-bearers of God in this world? This is your calling.

The home is also the place where those who will later run our nation are trained—or not trained. Do you want honest, upright, able men to guide our country's future? Those men are sitting in high chairs today in your dining room. They are digging trenches in the flowerbeds. If we do not want another generation of greedy, power-hungry politicians, we must nurture and train the leaders we desire within our own homes.

The home is also where future queens learn how to rule their own kingdoms. Are your daughters learning by example all that goes into the management of your family estate? It doesn't matter if you live in an apartment or in a grand house; your home is truly your family's castle. Do your daughters see you as queen and ruler of your realm or as a slave reluctantly doing enough to get by? The future of the home depends upon the example you are giving your daughters.

Our homes are also the frame for a very special picture that has been entrusted to Christian husbands and wives. Paul wrote that marriage is meant to be a picture of Christ and His Heavenly Bride, the Church. Our homes set the stage for this picture and for how it is presented to our world. Does your home reflect a wholehearted devotion to its King—your husbands and fathers? Does your home show a tender love and care for its Queen—all of you wives, mothers, and grandmothers? Your home can either lie about Christ and His Bride, or it can tell the truth. The truth is that the King provides for His Bride, lays down His life for her, and honors her with His own Body. The truth is that the Bride adores the King, delights in serving Him, and rejoices at His return.

Finally, the home is meant to welcome strangers and saints, to provide shelter, warmth, food—all the things that make up hospitality. Romans 12:13 says, "Share with God's people who are in need. Practice hospitality." I Peter 4:9 tells us to "Offer hospitality to one another without grumbling." The older women who are given as our examples in I Timothy 5 are commended for showing hospitality. Hospitality isn't about fancy dishes, nice tablecloths, five-course meals, or special occasions. Sure, there is a time and a place for all the nice table settings. We love to use them in our home, because they make a meal extra special. But hospitality can be shown with paper plates and sandwiches. The key element is an open heart, a loving home, and a willingness to serve others. Is your home open?

Exhortation for All Ages

Little girls, do you know that you have a special role God has made just for you? Do you know what a privilege it is to be a daughter in a Christian family? You have the opportunity to bless your parents while you are young that you might never have again. By your joyful obedience, you proclaim Christ to the world! You can bless your brothers and sisters by showing them kindness and practicing womanliness now, while you are still growing up. You can especially be a blessing to your mothers, helping them to fulfill their callings in showing hospitality, making home a haven, and demonstrating the love of Christ for His Church.

Wives, our world tells you daily that the best thing you can do to help your husband is to leave home and earn that second income. What is really sad is that our economy and our political structure have now been built around the model of the two-income family, often making it extremely difficult for a family to survive on a single income—or at least making it a sacrifice. It's considered "radical" today to declare that God created wives to serve their own husbands at home and that the wife at home has a vital role in the health of our culture and our nation. But your role isn't one your husband can easily replace. He can't just buy a "stay-at-home" robot—nor would such a machine be able to take over the tasks that are central to running a hospitable, welcoming, beautiful home.

Mothers, do you know what a priceless and irreplaceable role you have? No one else can fulfill your role. Oh, they can try, and today our society is structured around replacing mothers with daycare workers, "experts," and "professional childcare givers." But you really don't need studies or graphs or statistics to tell you what you already know deep down. Every child is different, and no one can love your child like you do. No one has your child's interests at heart like you do. And the bottom line is that God has not called anyone else to fulfill your role in bringing up your children to know Him, love Him, and obey Him.

Grandmothers, aunts, cousins, friends—do you know what a vital support role you have in God's kingdom? We all need your shining examples, your instruction, your patience, your experience. The Bible tells us that the older women who have successfully brought up godly children and created hospitable homes are to teach the younger women. Where are the older women today? Where are our teachers? We need you more than ever, because the skills, attitudes, and beliefs that you uphold will be lost if you do not pass them on.

I hope you are inspired to see that passing on a vision of godly womanhood is absolutely vital to the health of our families and the Church at large. I hope you will see how one faithful mother can have an impact that will affect generations. It is, after all, the little things that add up in the making of men and women. Holding a child on your lap, reading out loud, extending your hand to the elderly, listening to someone who needs a sympathetic ear—these things all add up as we work to build a culture of kindness, beauty, strength, and wisdom. Do you want to rule the world? Start ruling your homes!

Thank God, O women for the quietude of your home, and that you are queen in it. Men come at eventide to the home; but all day long you are there, beautifying it, sanctifying it, adorning it, blessing it. Better be there than wear a queen's coronet. Better be there than carry the purse of a princess. It may be a very humble home. There may be no carpet on the floor. There may be no pictures on the wall. There may be no silks in the wardrobe; but, by your faith in God, and your cheerful demeanor, you may garniture that place with more splendor than the upholsterer's hand ever kindled.

—*T. DeWitt Talmage*

Bear in mind that that woman is most queenly, who uses her wisdom and her strength for the benefit of those around her, shrinking from no duty that she should perform, but doing it cheerfully and well.

—*The King's Daughter and Other Stories for Girls*

Womanhood is a wonderful thing. In womankind we find the mothers of the race. There is no man so great, nor none sunk so low, but once he lay helpless, innocent babe in a woman's arms and was dependent upon her love and care for his existence. It is woman who rocks the cradle of the world and hold the first affections of mankind. She possesses a power beyond that of a king on his throne. . . . Womanhood stands for all that is pure and clean and noble. She who does not make the world better for having lived in it has failed to be all that a woman should be.

—Mabel Hale, *Beautiful Girlhood*

In Defense of Noble Womanhood
Proverbs 31:10-31
Given by the mother of King Lemuel to her son
by Rebecca Belcher Morecraft

For generations our culture has chosen to believe the lie that women and men should be considered "equal" in every way. We can date this fabrication back at least to the Woman's Suffragette Movement of the early 1900s, if not all the way back to Eve who chose to believe Satan rather than God. The separate roles God created in the beginning for each sex have largely been forgotten in modern times and substituted with a false idea of equality that in no way resembles God's original plan when He created woman from the rib of man and arranged for future humans to spring from the womb of woman, thus establishing a healthy "co-dependency" for the continuance of life.

Those who adhere to the world's ideas about womanhood point an accusing finger at stay-at-home women who have more than 1.5 children and no outside job. They believe the "old fashioned" wife and mother is "stuck" at home. Surely she must be discontented and ashamed of her plight in life. Their view from the wrong end of the telescope without the filtering lens of the Scriptures and read with unregenerate eyes, seems forlorn indeed. Apparently, her husband, though hard-working, is unsympathetic to her needs. He is often gone eight hours or more a day and only comes home to eat, sleep and father more children, it would seem. Her children obviously suck her dry by constant demands on her time and energy, until, alas, she can no longer fit the image of the successful woman of the times.

Just look at her! Her once slim, shapely figure is now sagging and stippled with broken veins. Her beautiful face, once radiant with the dew of youth, is now lined with care. Her once luxuriant hair has thinned and grayed. She no longer possesses boundless energy—her quick step has slowed to a determined pace. Although she is always combed and clean, her fashion sense seems stuck in a time warp with an emphasis on femininity and modesty. Clearly she is neglected and miserable and has no sense of "self-worth"!

Will she ever be able to break loose from this bondage and run free, prove her "true worth" and usefulness as she dresses in power suits and seductive fashions, becomes head of a corporation and makes men grovel? Only then will she gain respect from the world and perhaps make an appearance on Oprah to tell all about her struggles to the sympathetic thousands who will run to the nearest bookstore and buy her book. So says the world.

Observe true satisfaction! In contrast to the worldly-wise woman who is "ever learning, but never coming to a knowledge of the truth," examine the woman whose heart, mind, and body belong to Jesus. See the smile that curves the lips of the woman who writes "homemaker" on questionnaires as she watches her children grow into spiritually mature, productive adults who carry the eternal values they have learned from her into the future. How blessed is that woman whose home is full of the joyful chaos of many children!

Attest to radiant beauty as you see a life blessed by satisfaction in her noble calling as wife and mother! Full of kindness and grace, such a woman is an adornment to her husband. Place her on a pedestal, young women, rather than those whose manipulative whining and self-centered priorities may have coerced the lifestyle they crave to falsely beautify themselves but has brought them no satisfaction. The Christ-centered woman is able to walk with poise amongst the most elegantly attired, though her countenance is more sober than many. The beauty of holiness shines through the window of her eyes from a heart full of gratitude for God's grace and softened by griefs bravely borne. A deep contrition for her own sinfulness, coupled with the joy that flows from sins forgiven, radiates from her and blesses all who know her.

Attend to true wisdom! She holds in light regard all things but those that possess eternal value. Her perspectives and priorities, shaped by every Word that proceeds from the mouth of God, inform and beautify her life's callings. She daily increases her scope of learning because she knows that all truth, goodness, and beauty reflect her Creator/Redeemer. She learns what her gifts are and develops them to the further benefit of her husband, children, and the kingdom of Christ. Her choices and goals are not self-directed but Christ-directed as she seeks to do all to the glory of God. His Word informs and directs her behavior, her goals, and her conversation. She is dependable and consistent as she finds her focus each day, not in herself or others, but in Christ and His wisdom.

Mark true strength! She makes her arms strong physically by taking care of herself for the sake of Christ, her husband and children. In all humility, she recognizes that she has no strength in and of herself. Her core of endurance comes from her reliance on God who carries her through the trials of life and empowers her with His strength in her times of weakness. She smiles at the future, not because of her preparation alone, but because she trusts her strong Redeemer, Jehovah Jireh, to continue to supply her needs and those of her family as He ordains from His storehouse of riches in glory.

Learn sincere compassion. She is full of patience and compassion for those still walking in darkness as well as for her little ones who will learn love at her knee. She knows how and when to speak, with plainness and kindness, and can be patiently quiet. Heedless of scorn and disdain from those around her who do not know her Lord, she persists in rightly dividing the Word of Truth so that she will be ready with answers for those who ask, being bold as a lion and gentle as a dove. The law of kindness is always on her tongue. Her thoughtfulness and kindness of speech decorate her with such light and warmth that those who are cast about in a cold and heartless world may safely come to her to be warmed and fed. To be with her is to be nourished.

Stand amazed by her accomplishments! Her husband's love ennobles her. She seeks no higher calling than to be his companion and helper. Her children, who rise up and bless her, are of unquestioned righteous character, reflecting her teachings in their lives. Together, she and her husband shoot their children into the future, confident that the God Who planned their lives before the foundations of the earth was laid, will keep and use them as sharp arrows to pierce the hearts of His enemies and bring great increase to His Kingdom on earth.

The attractions of this world and those who devote their lives to obtaining them will pass off the scene and be replaced with the next generation's empty schemes, but the woman who fears the Lord, she shall be praised. Her works will follow her, not to her credit, nor would she have it so, but to the praise of His glorious grace Who holds her heart captive and makes her life count.

This is the woman after God's own heart. Although as sinners we will never attain to the perfections of God's goals for us as women, we can know the contentment and deep joy that comes from His grace abounding as we lay down our lives every day for those God has placed around us to serve. May we do all that God has called and gifted us to do for His glory alone.

Learn the ways of the godly woman described in Proverbs 31 by King Lemuel's mother and imitate her; for only then will you experience the nobility which God intended for you since long before you were created.

A Life Worth Living

Highest aim and true endeavor;
Earnest work, with patient might;
Hoping, trusting, singing ever;
Battling bravely for the right;
Loving God, all men forgiving;
Helping weaker feet to stand,—
These will make a life worth living,
Make it noble, make it grand.

Author Unknown

The Woman's Sphere
by John Angell James (excerpted from *Female Piety*, 1853)

[I]t will, perhaps, be asked, whether I would shut up every married woman within the domestic circle, and ... confine her to her own home; or whether I would condemn and degrade her to mere household drudgery. I have, I think, protected myself already from this imputation, by representing her as the companion, counselor, and comforter of man. She shall, with my consent, never sink from the side of man, to be trampled under his feet. She shall not have one ray of her glory extinguished, nor be deprived of a single honor that belongs to her sex; but to be the instructress of her children, the companion of her husband, and the queen partner of the domestic state, is no degradation—and she only is degraded who thinks so!

Christianity has provided a place for woman for which she is fitted, and in which she shines; but take her out of that place, and her luster pales and sheds a feeble and sickly ray! Or to change the metaphor, woman is a plant, which in its own greenhouse seclusion will put forth all its brilliant colors and all its sweet perfume; but remove it from the protection of its own floral home into the common garden and open field, where hardier flowers will grow and thrive—its beauty fades and its fragrance is diminished. Neither reason nor Christianity invites woman to the professor's chair, or conducts her to the lawyer's bar, or makes her welcome to the pulpit, or admits her to the place of the magistracy. Both exclude her . . .from the violence and evil of the military, the debates of the senate, and the pleadings of the forum. And they bid her beware how she lays aside the delicacy of her sex, and listens to any doctrines which claim new rights for her. . . .

The Bible gives her place of majesty and dignity in the domestic circle—the heart of her husband and the heart of her family. It is the female supremacy of that domain, where love, tenderness, refinement, thought and tender feeling preside. "It is the privilege of making her husband happy and honored, and her sons and daughters the ornaments of human society. It is the sphere of piety, prudence, diligence, in the domestic station, and a holy and devout life. It is the sphere that was occupied by Hannah, the mother of Samuel; by Elizabeth, the mother of John; by Eunice, the mother of Timothy; and by Mary, the mother of Jesus. It is the respect and esteem of mankind."

. . . A woman who fills well the sphere assigned to her, as a wife and mother; who trains up good citizens. . ., and good fathers and mothers of other families which are to spring from her own; and so from generation to generation in all but endless succession, need not complain that her sphere of action and her power of influence are too limited for female ambition to aspire to. The mothers of the wise and the good are the benefactresses of the human race.

What would be gained to woman's comfort, respectability, or usefulness, or to the welfare of society, and how much would be lost to each, by withdrawing her from her own appropriate sphere, and introducing her to that for which she has no adaptation? Who, but a few wild visionaries, and rash speculatists, and mistaken advocates of 'woman's rights', would take her from the home of her husband, of her children, and of her own heart—to wear out her strength, consume her time, and destroy her feminine excellence—in committee-rooms, on platforms, in mechanics' or philosophical institutions?

But may not woman, in every way in her power—benefit society by her talents and her influence? Certainly, in every legitimate way. Her sphere is clearly assigned to her by God. . . .Woman can be spared from the lecturer's chair, the platform of general convocation, and the scene of public business; but she cannot be spared from the hearth of her husband, and the circle of her children! Substitutes can be found for her in the one, but not in the other. In the bosom of domestic privacy she fulfills with truest dignity and faithfulness the first and highest obligations of her sex.

When Queens Ride By
by Olive White Fortenbacher

John and Jennie Mangrave had eager plans when they married and took over the old farm. But their great faith dwindled as the first years passed. John worked later and later in the evenings. Jennie took more and more of the heavy tasks upon her own shoulders and had no time for the home and children. They were no further on, and life had degenerated into a straining, hopeless struggle.

One hot afternoon, Jennie was loading baskets of tomatoes to take to town when the children came running to tell her there was a dressed-up lady at the kitchen door. Wearily she followed the children back and saw a woman in a gray tweed coat that seemed somehow to be a part of her brownish hair. She was not young, but she was beautiful! An aura of eager youth clung to her, a clean and exquisite freshness. The stranger in turn saw a young woman, haggard and weary. Her eyes looked hard and haunted. Her calico dress was shapeless and begrimed from her work.

Stranger (smiling): "How do you do? We ran our car into the shade of your lane to have our lunch and rest for a while. And I walked on up to buy a few apples, if you have them."

Jennie (grudgingly): "Won't you go in and sit down? I'll go and pick the apples."

Stranger: "May I go with you? I'd love to help pick them."

Jennie: "Why, I s'pose so. If you can get out there through the dirt." (She led the way along the unkempt path toward the orchard. She had never been so acutely conscious of the disorder about her. She reached the orchard and began to drag a long ladder from the fence to the apple tree.)

Stranger (crying out): "Oh, but you can't do that! It's too heavy. Please let me pick a few from the ground."

Jennie: "Heavy? This ladder? I wish I didn't ever lift anything heavier than this. After hoistin' bushel baskets of tomatoes onto a wagon, this feels light to me."

Stranger: "But do you think you should? Do you think it's right...? Why, that's a man's work!"

Jennie (furiously): "Right! Who are you to be askin' me whether I'm right or not? A person like you don't know what work is!"

Stranger (soothingly): "I'm sorry I annoyed you by saying that. If you were to tell me all about it—because I'm only a stranger—perhaps it would help. Why can't we sit down here and rest a minute?"

Jennie: "Rest? Me sit down to rest, an' the wagon loaded to go to town? It'll hurry me now to get back before dark."

Stranger: "Just take the time you would have spent picking the apples. I wish I could help you. Won't you tell me why you have to work so hard?"

Jennie (half sullenly): "There ain't much to tell, only that we ain't g'tting' ahead. Henry Davis is talkin' about foreclosin' on us if we don't soon pay some principal. The time of the mortgage is out this year, an' mebbe he won't renew it. And it ain't that I haven't done my part. I'm barely thirty, an' I might be fifty, I'm so weatherbeaten. That's the way I've worked."

Stranger: "And you think that has helped your husband?"

Jennie (sharply): "Helped him? Why wouldn't it help him?"

Stranger: "Men are such queer things, husbands especially. For instance, they want us to be economical, and yet they love to see us in pretty clothes. They need our work, and yet they want us to keep our youth and beauty. And sometimes they don't know themselves which they really want most. So we have to choose. That's what makes it so hard. Just after we were married, my husband decided to have his own business, so he started a very tiny one. I helped my husband in the store, but we would both be tired and discouraged after a hard day at the office and we didn't seem to be having any great success. The house got run down and dinner was always a hasty affair, and soon we both started complaining and bickering with each other. Finally, we decided that maybe I should stay at home and let him take care of his work at the office as best he could. And then I worked in my house to make it a clean, shining, happy place. My husband would come home dead-tired and discouraged, ready to give up the whole thing. But after he had eaten and sat in our bright little living room, and I had told him all the funny things I could invent about my day, I could see him change. By bedtime, he had his courage back, and by morning, he was all ready to go out and fight again. And at last he won."

(Jennie did not speak. She only regarded her guest with a half-resentful understanding.)

Stranger: "There was a queen once, who reigned in troubled days. And every time the country was on the brink of war and the people ready to fly into a panic, she would put on her showiest dress and take her court with her, and go hunting. And when the people would see her riding by, they were sure all was well with the government. So she tided over many a danger. And I've tried to be like her. Whenever a big crisis comes in my husband's business, or when he's discouraged, I put on my prettiest dress and get the best dinner I know how, or give a party! And somehow it seems to work. That's the woman's part, you know . . . to play the queen. . . ." (A faint "honk honk" came from the lane. The stranger started to her feet.) "That's my husband. I must go. Please don't bother about the apples. I'll just take a few from under the tree." (Taking some coins from her purse) "And give these to the children."

Jennie's thoughts were too confused for speech, but, as she watched the stranger's erect figure hurrying toward the lane, she remembered her words with the pain of anger.

Jennie: "Easy enough for her to set talkin' about queens! She never felt the work at her throat like a wolf. Talk about choosin! I haven't got no choice, I just got to keep on goin', like I always have. . . .

She stopped suddenly and picked up a fairy-like hanky of white linen that the stranger had dropped. Its faint, delicious fragrance made her think wistfully of strange, sweet things. Of gardens in the early summer dusk; of wide, fair rooms with the moonlight shining in them; of pretty women in beautiful dresses dancing, and men admiring them.

She, Jennie, had nothing of that. Everything about their lives, her's and John's was coarseness, soiled somehow by the dragging, endless labor of the days. Suppose . . . suppose . . . suppose she were to try doing what the stranger had said, suppose she spent her time on the house and let the outside work go. . . .

Jennie (with sudden resolution): "Mebbe I'm crazy, but I'm going to do it." Jennie brushed her hair, changed her shoes, and put on her one good dress. Then with something of the burning zeal of a fanatic, she attacked the confusion in the kitchen. Buy half-past four the room was clean. Now for supper! She decided upon fried ham and browned potatoes and apple sauce with hot biscuits and pie. With a spirit of daring recklessness, she spread the one white table cloth on the table.

The first pan of the flaky brown mounds had been withdrawn from the oven when Henry Davis' car came up the lane. Cold fear struck Jennie. He could be coming for only one thing. As she stood shaken, wondering how she would live through what the next hour would bring, she heard the words again, "There was a queen once. . . ."

Jennie (cordially): "Well, howd' you do, Mr. Davis? Come right in. I'm real glad to see you. Been quite a while since you was over."

Henry (embarrassed): "Why no, now , I won't go in. I just stopped to see John on a little matter of business. I'll just. . . ."

Jennie: "You'll come right in. John will be in from milkin' in a few minutes an' you can talk while you eat, both of you. I've supper just ready."

Henry: "Why, now I reckoned I'd just speak to John, an' then be gettin on."

Jennie: "They'll see you at home when you get there. You never tasted my hot biscuits with butter an' quince honey or you wouldn't take so much coaxin!" (Henry Davis came in and sat down in the big, clean kitchen. His eyes took in every homely detail of the orderly room.) "And how are things goin' with you, Mr. Davis?"

Henry: "Oh, so so. How are they with you?"

Jennie: "Why, just fine, Mr. Davis! It's been hard sleddin', but I sort of think the worst is over. We'll be 'round to pay that mortgage so fast come another year that you'll be surprised."

Henry: "Well, now, that's fine. I always wanted to see John make a success of the old place, but a man has to sort of watch his investments. . . . Well, now, I'm glad things are pickin' up a little."

Jennie felt as though a tight band at her throat had relaxed. At the kitchen door John stopped, staring blankly at the scene before him . . . at Jennie's moving about the bright table, chatting happily with Henry Davis! At Henry himself, his sharp features softened by an air of great satisfaction. At the sixth plate on the white cloth—Henry was staying for supper! But the silent depths of John's nature served him well. He made no comment. He merely shook hands with Henry Davis and then washed his face at the sink. Jennie arranged the savory dishes, and they sat down to supper. Henry seemed to grow more and more genial and expansive as he ate. So did John. By the time the pie was set before them, they were laughing over a joke Henry had heard at Grange meeting. As they rose from the table, Henry brought the conversation awkwardly around to his errand.

Jennie (quickly): "I told him, John, that the worst's over now, and we're g'ttin' on fine! I told him we'd be swampin' him pretty soon with payments. Ain't that right, John?"

John's mind was not analytical. He had been host at a delicious supper with his ancient adversary, whose sharp face was marvelously softened. Jennie's eyes were shining with a new and amazing confidence. It was a natural moment for unreasoning optimism.

John: "Why, that's right, Mr. Davis. I believe we can start clearin' this off now pretty soon. If you could just see your way clear to renew the mortgage."

It was done. The papers were back in Davis' pocket. They had bid him a cordial good-bye from the door. Jennie cleared off the table and began to wash the dishes. John was fumbling through the papers on a hanging shelf. He finally sat down with an old tablet and pencil.

John: "I believe I'll do a little figurin' since I've got time tonight. It just struck me if I used my head a little more, I'll get on faster."

Jennie: "Well, now you might." (She polished two big apples and placed them on a saucer beside him.)

John (pleased): "Now that's what I like. Say, you look sort of pretty tonight."

Jennie (smiling): "Go along with you." But a wave of color swept up in her sallow cheeks. John had looked more grateful over her setting those two apples beside him now than he had the day last fall when she had lifted all the potatoes herself! Maybe even John had been needing something else more than he had needed the hard, back-breaking work she had been giving him!

Jennie walked to the doorway and stood looking off through the darkness. A thin, haunting breath of sweetness rose from the bosom of her dress where she had tucked the scrap of white linen. She wished that she could somehow tell the beautiful stranger that her words had been true . . . that she, Jennie, was going to fulfill her woman's part. She had read the real needs of John's soul from his eyes that evening. Yes, wives had to choose for their husbands sometimes.

At that very moment, speeding along the sleek macadam highway, a woman in a gray coat with a soft gray hat and a rose quill leaned suddenly close to her husband.

Husband: "Tired?"

Wife: "I'm all right. Only, only I can't get that poor woman at the farm out of my mind. It, it was so hopeless."

Husband (smiling tenderly): "Well, I'm sorry too, but you mustn't worry. Good gracious, darling, you're not weeping over it, I hope!"

Wife: "No, truly, just two little tears. I know it's silly, but I did so want to help her and I know that what I said sounded insane. She wouldn't know what I was talking about. She just looked up with that blank, tired face. And it all seemed so impossible. No . . . I'm not going to cry. Of course, I'm not . . . but . . . lend me your handkerchief, will you dear? I've lost mine somehow. . . ."

In our current culture, home has become so neglected that many people haven't the slightest idea what its purpose is outside of a place to sleep, relax, and sometimes eat. Home has lost its noble place in society so much so that people can't imagine what there is to do there all day long. Any woman who dares consider staying home full-time is made out to be a unintelligent woman living with half her brain tied behind her back.

Whatever happened to home being the center of the family, a haven of refreshment, a thriving metropolis of productivity? Instead, we have elaborate McMansions that are devoid of life. They might look pretty to the observer (thanks to hired maids and interior decorators), but they are usually just houses, not homes. They sit there empty and lifeless while the occupants live a hectic, frenetic, 100-mile-an-hour life in the fast lane—trying to get ahead, trying to get to the top of the corporate ladder, trying to squish in as many activities as can possibly be had outside the home.

We don't have to follow along in this madness. Our families deserve something better—they deserve a beautiful, welcoming home which is the heart of the family and the center for outreach to the world. Maybe our home isn't furnished very expensively and maybe it isn't very big, but we can do our best to recapture the nobility and rightful place of home in our society, beginning with our own home.

—Crystal Paine

Mothers and daughters, wives and sisters, remember that you have the making of the future of this great country, and rise at once to your high and holy duty. Remember that you must make that future, whether you will or not. We are all what you make us. Ah! Throw away your weakening follies of fashion, and soul-famine, and rise to the level where God intended you should be, and make every one of your homes, from this day, schools of true politeness and tender affection. Take those little curly-headed boys, and teach them all you would have them to be. They will be just such men, and will go forth to bless the world, and crown you with a glory such as queens and empresses never dreamed of. Exercise your power now, and you shall reap the fruit in your ripe age.

—*Daughters of Destiny*

I long to accomplish great and noble tasks, but it is my chief duty to accomplish humble tasks as though they were great and noble. The world is moved along, not only by the mighty shoves of its heroes, but also by the aggregate of the tiny pushes of each honest worker.

—*Helen Keller*

The modern challenge to motherhood is the eternal challenge—that of being a godly woman. The very phrase sounds strange in our ears. We never hear it now. We hear about every other type of women: beautiful women, smart women, sophisticated women, career women, talented women, divorced women. But so seldom do we hear of a godly woman—or of a godly man either, for that matter. I believe women come nearer to fulfilling their God given function in the home than anywhere else. It is a much nobler thing to be a good wife, than to be Miss America. It is a greater achievement to establish a Christian home than it is to produce a second rate novel filled with filth. It is a far, far better thing in the realms of morals to be old fashioned, than to be ultra-modern. The world has enough women who know how to be smart. It needs women who are willing to be simple. The world has enough women who know how to be brilliant. It needs some who will be brave. The world has enough women who are popular. It needs more who are pure. We need women, and men, too, who would rather be morally right than socially correct.

—Peter Marshall, former Chaplain
to the United States Senate

Believing that the intelligent, refined, modest Christian women were the real custodians of national purity, and the sole agents who could arrest the tide of demoralization breaking over the land, she [Edna]

addressed herself to the wives, mothers, and daughters of America; calling upon them to smite their false gods, and purify their shrines at which they worshiped. Jealously she contended for every woman's right which God and nature had decreed her sex. The right to be learned, wise, noble, useful, in woman's divinely limited sphere. The right to influence and exalt the circle in which she moved. The right to mount the sanctified beam of her own quiet hearth-stone; the right to modify and direct her husband's opinion, if he considered her worthy and competent to guide him; the right to make her children ornaments to their nation, and a crown of glory to their [people]; the right to advise, to plead, to pray . . . the right to be all the phrase 'noble Christian woman' means.

—*Augusta Jane Evans,* St. Elmo

To a certain extent, woman is the conservator of her nation's welfare. Her virtue, if firm and uncorrupted will stand sentinel over that empire.

—*John Angell James,* Female Piety, *1853*

The Need of the Hour

What does the country need? Not armies standing
With sabers gleaming ready for the fight;

Not increased navies, skillful and commanding,
To bound the waters with an iron might;
Not haughty men with glutted purses trying
To purchase souls, and keep the power of place;
Not jeweled dolls with one another vying
For palms of beauty, elegance, and grace.

But we want women, strong of soul, yet lowly
With that rare meekness, born of gentleness;
Women whose lives are pure and clean and holy,
The women whom all little children bless;
Brave, earnest women, helpful to each other,
With finest scorn for all things low and mean;
Women who hold the names of wife and mother
Far nobler than the title of a queen.

Oh! These are they who mold the men of story,
These mothers, oftime shorn of grace and youth,
Who, worn and weary, ask no greater glory
Than making some young soul the home of truth;
Who sow in hearts all fallow for the sowing
The seeds of virtue and of scorn for sin,
And, patient, watch the beauteous harvest growing
And weed out tares which crafty hands cast in.

Women who do not hold the gift of beauty
As some rare treasure to be bought and sold,
But guard it as a precious aid to duty—
The outer framing of the inner gold;
Women who, low above their cradles bending,

Let flattery's voice go by, and give no heed,
While their pure prayers like incense are ascending
These are our country's pride, our country's need.

Ella Wheeler Wilcox

Who can find a virtuous woman? for her price is far above rubies. The heart of her husband doth safely trust in her, so that he shall have no need of spoil. She will do him good and not evil all the days of her life. She seeketh wool, and flax, and worketh willingly with her hands. She is like the merchants' ships; she bringeth her food from afar. She riseth also while it is yet night, and giveth meat to her household, and a portion to her maidens. She considereth a field, and buyeth it: with the fruit of her hands she planteth a vineyard. She girdeth her loins with strength, and strengtheneth her arms. She perceiveth that her merchandise is good: her candle goeth not out by night. She layeth her hands to the spindle, and her hands hold the distaff. She stretcheth out her hand to the poor; yea, she reacheth forth her hands to the needy. She is not afraid of the snow for her household: for all her household are clothed with scarlet. She maketh herself coverings of tapestry; her clothing is silk and purple. Her husband is known in the gates, when he sitteth among the elders of the land. She maketh fine linen, and selleth it; and delivereth girdles unto the

merchant. Strength and honour are her clothing; and she shall rejoice in time to come. She openeth her mouth with wisdom; and in her tongue is the law of kindness. She looketh well to the ways of her household, and eateth not the bread of idleness. Her children arise up, and call her blessed; her husband also, and he praiseth her. Many daughters have done virtuously, but thou excellest them all. Favour is deceitful, and beauty is vain: but a woman that feareth the LORD, she shall be praised. Give her of the fruit of her hands; and let her own works praise her in the gates. (Proverbs 31:10-31)

Women of Vision
By Jennie Chancey

I am not here to serve myself. I am not here to be lauded, petted, admired or "affirmed." I am here to build men, cultures and kingdoms. When I find myself in the midst of difficulties and pain, will I persevere, or will I become a coward and pity myself? We do not have time for self-pity! We have much to do, and the hour is late! We need a broader vision of home than just ourselves as wives and mothers, sisters and daughters. We need to understand that we are at work to build Christ's kingdom —for eternity! It isn't just about children who sit politely at the supper table and stand obediently with mama in the grocery store. It isn't just about homes that sparkle with cleanliness. It isn't just about spouses who love one another and present a glorious picture of Christ and His bride, the Church, although these things are certainly important. It is all these things coming together to build a culture. Do we have the vision for this, or is our focus on the dirty dishes and unfolded laundry of life?

Little girls, do you have a vision for serving your parents at home? Do you have a vision for serving Christ by doing loving acts of obedience and helping around your home? Or do you gripe about all the work there is to do and wonder when you can get out of it or get some appreciation for all of it. Christ said to his apostles, "If anyone desires to be first, he shall be last of all and servant of all" (Mark 9:35). He also told them, that at the judgment, "many who are first will be last, and the last first" (Mark 10:31). People that we thought were the greatest in this world will be considered last when it comes time to have their works weighed at Christ's throne. And many we wouldn't even have noticed will be made first in the kingdom of God. Are we willing to be last and least now? Are we willing to be the "servant of all?" We have Christ as our example!

When the disciples looked for a conquering king, Christ bent down to wash their feet, saying, "Do you know what I have done to you? You call Me Teacher and Lord, and you say well, for so I am. If I then, your Lord and Teacher, have washed your feet, you also ought to wash one another's feet. For I have given you an example, that you should do as I have done to you. Most assuredly,

I say to you, a servant is not greater than his master; nor is he who is sent greater than he who sent him. If you know these things, blessed are you if you do them" (John 13:12-17). Let this penetrate your being until it becomes a part of who you are: It is not the served, but the servant, who is counted the greatest in the kingdom of God! This is grace! This is joy!

To the unsaved, this is, of course, rank foolishness. "For pity's sake!" they cry, "Stop all this groveling and serving and get a life for yourself! Find yourself! Make a name for yourself! There is more to life than washing other people's feet and wiping little noses and bottoms! There is more to life than following someone else's lead! Get out there and lead yourself!" I get notes like these all the time from visitors to my Ladies Against Feminism web site. They feel we have bought into a terrible lie that will "hold us down" as women for centuries to come. They think we are advocating a return to the Dark Ages. What they cannot understand is that every person in this world is a servant to someone. No one is out from under authority! The woman in an office is still under a boss. Even a CEO has to answer to the owner of the company and the owner to the stockholders. And the person who thinks he is completely free from anyone else is still a servant to himself! Will we be slaves to our own passions, or will we be slaves to Christ? There is no neutrality. There is no other choice.

Paul writes, "For you were bought at a price; therefore glorify God in your body and in your spirit, which are God's" (I Cor. 6:10). Later he writes, "You were bought at a price; do not become slaves of men" (I Cor. 7:23). We are not our own. We belong to the One who paid the ultimate price for us. The shed blood of Christ covers our sins. What a payment! We can never be worthy of such a price. Paul tells us in Romans 6:18, "[H]aving been set free from sin, you became slaves of righteousness." Yet, at the same time, Christ calls us friends: "No longer do I call you servants, for a servant does not know what his master is doing; but I have called you friends, for all things that I heard from My Father I have made known to you" (John 15:15). Isn't this exciting? We are a part of the kingdom-building vision of Christ, and He has shared the vision with us—not hiding it from us as if we were dumb animals harnessed to the plow.

Our question now must be, will we serve? Will we continue to press on and win the race? Will we see our work for what it is—a multigenerational plan to build Christ's kingdom, advance the gospel and create beautiful cultures? Or will we become shortsighted and narrow in our vision, like a mule behind blinders? Will we complain that we do not receive the recognition we "deserve" in this life? What can that recognition matter when we are aiming for the prize of Christ's "Well done, thou good and faithful servant?"

Little girls, do you see your work in your homes—

all that mopping, dusting, dishwashing and picking up after others—as a glorious work of kingdom building for Christ? Mothers, do you see yourselves as queens in this kingdom or as drones? You decide upon your attitude— no one else does it for you. We do not have time to let circumstances dictate our response to life. We must allow Christ to dictate our response to the circumstances we face! Feminism isn't what shouts at you from a NOW convention or a pro-abortion rally. Feminism isn't the radicals demanding "no-fault" divorces and free state-run daycare. Feminism is the face that looks back at you in the mirror and says, "The grass is greener on the other side. Take, eat of this apple. God is hiding something from you that you deserve." And the only way to combat that spirit of Eve is to look it in the face, acknowledge that culture-killing sin as our own and fight it with the Word of God. "It is written!" Christ cried. "It is written!" The Word of God tells me what I am to be as a woman. The Word of God shows me that to be the greatest of all, I must become the least and the last. And, incredibly enough, the Word of God reveals that there is joy, satisfaction and peace in this life of service! I am here to testify that it is real. His Holy Spirit is our comforter and will not forsake us. He is with us!

Mothers, take heart. You are building cultures, societies and kingdoms while you are training those little people within your home. No matter what, someone is going to train them. Our rotten culture didn't come out of nowhere. It came because Christian families forsook their first duty and abandoned their homes to the enemy. Let us return to our homes and rebuild a vision for godly descendants that stretches into the future.

Sisters and daughters, take heart. You are helping to create the world that we will inhabit tomorrow. There is nothing insignificant about the work you do in your family and your home. Loving your siblings is a glorious work unto the Lord. Responding with joy and delight to the tasks set before you is vitally important! Let no one fool you: What you do every day makes a difference in the world for good or ill.

Grandmothers, aunts and cousins, you are a part of this vision, too! It is a lie that only mothers of children can affect the future. We are all part of a Body that needs each member. The arm cannot say to the eye, "I don't need you; I can do this work myself." We must all pull together to accomplish the job that Christ has laid before us. I need the encouragement and guidance of my older sisters in Christ. I need the servant-hearted help of my younger sisters in Christ. We are a Body! We are in this together!

If we want to see our culture redeemed and made beautiful and pure once again, we must return to the "old paths" spoken of in Jeremiah 6:16. It is only there that we will "find rest for our souls." We must be willing to be considered foolish by the world. We must be willing to die to self. It is only when we die that we find true life. This "foolishness" is the wisdom of God! If we want wholehearted womanhood to become reality again, we must be willing to forsake the glittering paths of fame, recognition and celebrity. If we want beautiful girlhood for our young ladies—a time of innocence, joy and delight in service—then we must be willing to demonstrate it in our own homes and live it beautifully for the watching world.

We are daughters of the King! We are building a kingdom that will have no end. We are shaping cultures—for good or ill—as we go about our daily tasks. Let us purpose to follow Christ wholeheartedly, embracing the servanthood He demonstrated to us. Let us purpose to put to death the grasping desire for fame that our godless culture has raised up as its idol. Let us be women of purpose and vision, serving Christ from hearts that overflow with love for His people and for the lost.

CHAPTER TWO

The King's Daughters

The king's daughter is all glorious within. . .
(Psalm 45:13)

. . .That our daughters may be as corner stones, polished after the similitude of a palace. . . (Psalm 144:12)

Kings' daughters were among thy honourable women. . .
(Psalm 45:9)

Many daughters have done virtuously, but thou excellest them all. (Proverbs 31:29)

Daughters at Home
by Stacy McDonald

What is a corner stone?

A cornerstone is the foundational stone at the corner of two walls. It is not used in just any structure, but is typically found in temples, churches, mansions, or elaborate buildings. A cornerstone is set in a prominent location and typically has an inscription that communicates to others the details of the structure's history.

So by looking at the cornerstone you should know who designed the structure, how old it is, who built it, who owns it and possibly what its worth as a historical monument.

Other Bible versions use the word pillar. "That our daughters may be as pillars, sculptured in palace style. . . ." What is a pillar? A pillar can either provide a strong foundational support to whatever is above it or it can stand alone as a monument. Typically, it supports something. (Interesting that our daughters may be later called to be helpmeets to their husbands who are in authority over them).

The psalmist says the pillar is sculptured in palace style. In other words the pillar has been carefully cut, shaped, and polished to be fit for a palace—for royalty. This is a picture of how we are to raise our daughters—to be fit for glorifying the King of kings in whatever way he wishes.

When the world sees our daughters, they should see strong pillars of faithful purity and beauty. A godly maiden is a living testimony to her Creator—she amplifies not herself, but God. Supporting and serving not herself, but her family and those who God calls her to serve.

The world would like to teach our daughters that their beauty is measured by how much they weigh and how sensually attractive they are—that old age is their biggest enemy. The world rages that a daughter should live for herself, become as independent and powerful as she can, and, "above all," they tell her, "never let a man rule your life."

For the record, a maiden isn't called to be weak or helpless; she is literally to be a pillar of strength—His strength. She is also to be beautiful—to radiate His beauty with all purity and love. She obtains this type of loveliness through His faithful craftsmanship of her character and demeanor; not from her own vain efforts at the fading kind of beauty—though her outward appearance in not unimportant.

Our daughters are to be molded, shaped, and polished so they are strong cornerstones who actively glorify God and stand as a steadfast testimony to future generations. They are to be fully able to support that which they have been called to bear with dignity, virtue, and strength.

Interestingly, a maiden's testimony bears the holy inscription of the One to Whom she belongs. And since she is not her own, but she is bought with a price, her very life should vibrantly declare the glory of her Creator.

A princess is a royal noblewoman, a ruler's daughter or wife who honors all aspects of her inheritance and discharges her duties with grace and royal bearing, serving her people and leading them to positions of greater blessing. She recognizes that all thrones must be established in righteousness and that she must defend the faith and strengthen the morality of her people by her public and private example. In this generation that is starving for examples of femininity, modesty, and true princess-like behavior, we must be the examples.

A girl can be her father's arrow and a cultural leader while under her father's roof and protection by setting an example of something which is almost a thing of the past: virtuous daughterhood.

—*Anna Sofia Botkin*

Daughters as Pillars
by June Fuentes

Graceful and beautiful pillars are indeed being raised today. I have seen them with my own eyes. They stand out from the crowd. They are being raised for kingdom purposes. Theirs is a strong and sacred foundation—the Holy Scriptures. This is where they are learning the character of the Proverbs 31 women and the mandates of Titus 2:4-6:

1. Learning to love their future husbands
2. Learning to love their future children
3. To be self-controlled
4. To be pure
5. To be keepers at home
6. To be kind
7. Learning to be subject to their future husbands so the word of God will not be maligned

This new generation of daughters is being raised to fear the Lord. They are taught to be feminine women of nobility, courage, diligence, loyalty and submission. They esteem purity and modesty. They strive to be honorable. They are daughters who have vision and remarkable influence as they help to advance the kingdom of God. These daughters have given their hearts to their parents and desire to help and bless them and their families. They learn the value of a meek and quiet spirit as they firmly defend and teach the Word to all who are willing to listen. They know their true purpose because they are serving the Lord wholeheartedly. They embrace how they were designed to be help-meets and seek to be industrious to help their fathers and future husbands. Many are highly educated and well-equipped to teach the next generation about the Lord and prepare for Him an army of warriors.

Godly daughters follow in the spirit of Psalm 144:12 and Titus 2. They are pillars and cornerstones, which is another word often used in this verse, help to support and vital in maintaining a buildings structure. Much in the same way daughters become just as invaluable to a home as they grow and help it to run successfully. Godly daughter's embrace their father's vision and take it up as their own. Virtuous daughters being brought up to be godly women are invaluably priceless in the eye's of the Lord (Proverbs 31:10), and they impact society and culture with a powerful rippling effect.

So, dear Christian Mothers, know that that little daughter sitting next to you is cherished in the Lord's eyes. The babes she will raise will be the next generation which will serve Him. She will be standing shoulder-to-shoulder with her husband taking dominion and quite possibly be at the helm with him, leading the future church, mentoring men and women alike as they take their place in reforming culture. She will be making strong the fabric of society by taking her place in the home and in her family, making it an example for others to learn from and to bring God glory. Be careful to guide her and protect her. Be careful to teach her all that you know and much, much more. Love her with the love that comes from the Heavenly Father and be found trustworthy of discipling her well.

The best monument for grateful affection to erect is a noble, beautiful life, a joy to the heart and an honor in the eyes of fond parental hope...

If children would do their part well in return for all the love that has blessed their helpless years and surrounded them in their youth, and that lingers still unwasted in the days of manhood and womanhood, they must seek to realize in their own lives all the sacred hopes of their parents' hearts. A wrecked and debauched manhood or a frivolous and purposeless womanhood is a poor return for parental love, fidelity and sacrifice. But a noble life, a character strong, true, earnest and Christlike, brings blessed and satisfying reward to a parent for the most toilsome and painful years of self forgetting love. Parents live in their children, and children hold in their hands the happiness of their parents. Let them never be untrue to their sacred trust. Let them never bring down the gray hairs of father or mother with sorrow to the grave. Let them be worthy of the love, almost divine, that holds them in its deathless grasp. Let them so live as to be a crown of honor to their parents in their old age.

—J.R. Miller, The Family, 1882

Seasons of Daughterhood
by Rebecca Serven Loomis

"And may our daughters be like palace cornerstones . . ."

—Psalm 144:12b,
The Book of Psalms for Singing

Contemplating the name "Daughter" conjures up scenes of a freckle-faced, pig-tailed girl grinning right straight up at you. But the season of daughterhood, growing from princess to queen, encompasses far more than those typically thought of years.

Starting young, the wee lass wails, tiny fuzz adorning her head. She does not even understand her title, yet unconsciously rests in it by the sacrificial love of her parents.

As she grows, petticoats and pantalets beautify the young princesses' frame. Wildflowers decorate her escapades, while mud pies fill her days. Her parents lead her along in the ways she should go: teaching her to share toys with her little brother, help mommy do the dishes, listen to daddy read the Bible, play with grandpa in the autumn leaves. She lisps her first prayers, memorizes her first verses of Scripture, and begins to learn about her God.

The daughter matures again, sounding out the ABC's with the purpose of reading God's Word. She counts numbers with the aim of inculcating good stewardship. She slowly grasps the meaning of sin and repentance, the Lord working within her heart, and drawing her unto Himself.

The girl starts to recognize what it means to be a blessing to her family, as she reads stories to her sister, or creates that first juicy berry pie for her daddy with mommy's assistance. She faithfully builds relationships with her parents, her siblings, and her God.

As vice regents over the domestic reign, her parents lovingly give her encouragement and the daughter learns to embrace their vision. Looking beyond her parent's verbalized direction, she takes initiative and surprises them, doing things she knows would please them. Smiling cheerfully, she washes the dishes. Developing her interests to bless others and glorify the Lord, she writes letters of encouragement to young and old, or grows blooms for the dinner meal. She dies to herself, seeking to bring honor to her parents. Especially when she sees their imperfections and inconsistencies, she purposes to love them as Christ loves her.

Joining in the conversation, the girl becomes a noble woman. She serves as an integral part of her family whether that is her father's house or husband's. The daughter, now stately in the bloom of womanhood, joys in life with vigor in the Lord.

Thoughtful eyes discern the little one's needs. Instructive discipline sees the big picture for growth in the children. Listening ears are ready at a moments notice to drop all and be there for a needy soul. Yummy meals, elegant in their simplicity, grace her table. She serves without thanks, out of love for her Redeemer, Jesus Christ. As she dons her apron, rolling up her sleeves to embrace each task, she exemplifies sturdy virtue. Surrounded by little ones gazing up at her, she seeks to emulate the honor towards her parents that the children must embrace as ones who serve their King.

No matter what her station, be it married or maiden, she still seeks to honor her "goodly inheritance." For through far from perfect, her journey through life is her very own providential history, full of joys and bitter sadness, hope, and love, and faith in God.

All through life she remains a queenly daughter; serving, honoring her kin who gave her life. With a few hairs of gray sneaking around her temple, and joys and sorrows of the years leave their trace on the daughter's face, she acquires a comfortable beauty of age. Cookies, phone calls, visits to "the homestead", letters, hugs and kisses, talks late into the night; she gleans wisdom as her parents give it, seeking to honor with all her might.

Even when her parents approach the River, anticipating their passage to eternity, the daughter lovingly remains beside them; caring, overlooking faults, persevering with wisdom through the tough days, treasuring each moment. She builds memories for the young ones around her, be it children or grandchildren, nieces or nephews.

Throughout each stage of her life, she strives by God's grace to be an honoring daughter. She prays that when her parents leave her, the Lord will look at her, His daughter, now bedecked with locks of gray, and say, "Well done, my good and faithful daughter." And she will joy in what the Lord has done.

Some women are grandmothers. Some women are mothers. Some women are wives. But all women are daughters. Live your life as a grateful daughter, nobly serving, to bring joy to your Father's heart.

A Princess she, though not by birth:
Her title's from above,
Her heritage the right of worth,
Her empire that of love.

Author Unknown

To those intrepid English women whose courage, fortitude and devotion brought a new nation into being, this statue of the Pilgrim Maiden is dedicated.

—Inscription on the Pilgrim Maiden's
Monument in Plymouth, MA

Letter to a Twelve-Year-Old Girl
by Anna Sofia & Elizabeth Botkin

Dear _____,

Congratulations on entering another year to spend in the Lord's service!

You are embarking on a monumental season in your life—the season of transition from beautiful girlhood to noble womanhood. Don't ever think that this time in your life is less important, or that the decisions you will make will have less significance, than when you begin the season of wifehood and motherhood.

We do not know you, though we wish we did, and so we write this letter as though we were writing it to our twelve-year-old selves, filling it with the admonition and encouragement that we so needed. As we write this letter, we have just turned 21 and 19, but those years are fresh in our minds, as are the joys, the struggles, the spiritual victories, the failures, the moral tests, the decisions and the mistakes of those years that molded our character and made us the women that write to you today. When you are 21, what will you remember of your 12th year? What regrets do you not want to have? What victories do you want to tell your children about? What testimonies of God's sanctifying grace will people see in you?

Your mother told us that you have a sensitive heart that loves the Lord. This is the finest quality a girl can possess. It will be your guard against the host of distractions and temptations that will arise during this season. The next few years will bring new levels of wisdom and experience and of the knowledge of good and evil, and a stronger awareness of our "crooked and perverse generation." Two things will help you keep your heart pure and enable you to see evil with the Lord's eyes:

- Immerse yourself in the Scriptures and pray that God will give you purity and wisdom.

- Cultivate gratitude and honor for your parents; turn your eyes to them and seek their instruction with all your heart.

My son, keep your father's command, and do not forsake the law of your mother. Bind them continually upon your heart; tie them around your neck. When you roam, they will lead you; when you sleep, they will keep you; and when you awake, they will speak with you. For the commandment is a lamp, and the law is a light; reproofs of instruction are the way of life. . . . (Proverbs 6:20-23)

At your age, most girls become more aware of the need built into them for male affection, love and protection. You must learn to cherish the father that God gave you, as your confidant, friend, knight in shining armor, protector and guardian, and look to him to provide the security and love that you need, until the time comes that he gives you in marriage. Adore him, pray for him, ask him questions, and let him know that you are behind him in everything he does. Pray with him for your future husband.

These are establishing years. Your character is still soft and impressionable, and your mind is still tender. Use these years to establish virtuous character and good habits, and you will render yourself more useful to your Maker.

Don't destroy your good sense by putting worthless things before your eyes (Psalm 101:3). Don't waste your youth and corrupt your mind by allowing the wrong influences to leave permanent impressions on it. Be careful of trifles that may give you an appetite for pettiness— novels, silly friends, films that glorify immaturity, useless and unedifying conversations, daydreams, and all other vanities.

One thing that will compromise your usefulness to God is a socially-debilitating self-consciousness, all too common in young ladies. We have both known what it is to be consumed with awkwardness and nervousness in public. This tendency comes from an absorbing focus on self and a fear of man. You must cultivate a greater fear of God to triumph over your fear of man, and a love of others to conquer your interest in yourself.

Twelve is not too young to develop the manners of a lady. The heart of ladylike conduct is not strict adherence to a list of social rules, but rather a genuine love of others and concern for their comfort. A true lady's conduct transcends her age and situation. Be gracious, hospitable, and interested in people of all ages, and represent your Heavenly Father with grace and nobility.

You would be blessed by pursuing relationships with older girls you have reason to respect; these friendships would likely be more fruitful and edifying than friendships only with girls your own age. Don't let shyness stop you from initiating such friendships; as older girls, we can assure you that we and our peers would be honored and touched, and impressed, by the attention of younger girls. 1 Timothy 4:12 admonishes us, "Let no man despise thy youth; but be thou an example of the believers, in word, in conversation, in charity, in spirit, in faith, in purity." Some of the most edifying and God-honoring conversations we've ever had have been with girls your age.

As our final encouragement, don't underestimate the influence God has given you by putting you in a godly Christian family. Your faithful service within your family is a powerful testimony that can have world-wide impact and will touch generations to come.

This is a glorious time to be a daughter. May our wonderful Lord bless you richly and use you mightily.

Your sisters in Christ,
Anna Sofia and Elizabeth Botkin

A Word to Sisters
by J.R. Miller, excerpted from *The Family*, 1882

May I try to tell you, dear girls, how you can indeed be your brothers' guardian angels? Show them in your own lives at home the perfect grace and beauty of a true, noble, and lofty womanhood. Strive after all that is delicate, all that is pure, all that is tender, all that is holy and sacred in the divine ideal of womanhood. Show them in yourselves such perfect loveliness that they will turn away ever after from everything that is unlovely. Make virtue so attractive to them, as they see it embodied in you, that they will always be repelled by vice. Let them see in you such purity of soul, such sweetness of spirit, such divine sanctity, that wherever they go your influence will hang about them like an armor of defense, or, like an angel, hover above their heads in perpetual benediction. Be as nearly a perfect woman, each one of you, through Christ's help, as it is possible for you to be. Then when temptations come to your brother there will rise up before his eyes such visions of purity and love that he will turn away with loathing from the tempter. . . .

If you will only be true, noble, unselfish, gentle, womanly, in the highest, purest sense; if you only are thoughtful and considerate and live for a purpose, making your character decided and strong, you will throw over your brothers a silent, imperceptible yet mighty influence, which will be a shield to them in danger, a panoply in temptation, and which will fill their hearts with the purest, loftiest aspirations and aims.

Next to mother and father, there is no one who can do so much to help a young man to live nobly as his own sister. She cannot always go with him. Her weak arm could not always shield him if she were beside him. But there is a help which she can give him that will prove mightier than her presence. It is not the help of good advice and earnest words—these should have power, too—but the help rather of silent and holy influence, gained in the home by a life of unselfishness and beauty, and then held as a potent charm outside and beyond the home walls. There is a power over her brother possible to every true sister, which would be like the very hand of God to guide him and restrain him in all the paths of life.

After years of society belittling the calling of motherhood, something wonderful is happening—something wonderfully counter-cultural! In the midst of the anti-life, anti-motherhood philosophies which pervade the culture, there is a new generation of young ladies whose priorities are not determined by the world's expectations of them. They have grown up in homes where fathers shepherded them, where children are not merely welcomed, but where they are deeply loved. Some of these women have been home educated, which means that many of them have grown up around babies and their mothers. They have learned to see motherhood as a joy and a high calling because their parents see it that way.

When asked about their future, these girls know their own minds. These are the future mothers of the Church: Young women who are not afraid to say that the goal of all of their education and training is to equip them to pursue the highest calling of womanhood—the office of wife and mother.

—Douglas Phillips

Keepers-at-Home: The Highest Calling
By Elizabeth Serven Ten Dolle, Originally written in 2003. Elizabeth is now a happy wife and the mother of a baby girl.

Throughout the last several months I have been continually interrogated regarding my future plans. I have been tempted to answer many different ways. For example, "I'll be attending Scubadiving School off the coast of Maine." Or "I have landed a job in Brazil raising purebred alpacas." But as I have considered it more I don't think I like swimming all that much and Brazil is awfully humid. Hmmm. . . . I could just stay here and flip burgers at McDonald's. . . . It is actually easier to say some of these outlandish ideas than to admit what my real calling should be. Yet if God calls women to be keepers-at-home, I believe all young women should be preparing with the same purpose in mind.

Some people might imagine today's woman at home, lying on her plush sofa and eating bon-bons with nothing to do. After all, we have so many modern timesaving conveniences. But there actually is much work that needs to be done at our time of history. As a young woman, in this time of preparation, shouldn't we also be in the home? This is certainly not a second-rate job that I am pursuing! I will have the opportunity to impact generations to come—people that I may never meet—by faithfully fulfilling the calling of wife and mother.

My preparation may include how to scramble an egg. . . but also how to prepare nutritious and appetizing food that will sustain those who gather around my table; encouraging them to linger, wrestle with ideas, and have new vision for what the Lord has called them to do. I desire for that table to be a significant place of discipleship, hospitality and evangelism. My preparation may include washing windows and mopping floors. . . but also making a home a haven of rest for my family as well as our guests. I hope to create lovely surroundings, where others are able to rejoice in the life that the Lord has given them and to be rejuvenated.

My preparation may include changing diapers and washing clothes. . . but it is also cultivating a heart for children. Leading them and loving them so that they grow to be healthy members of God's kingdom. Teaching each little one to live a life that will glorify the Lord and to obey His word, thereby establishing future generations in their callings. This is the most significant work of all.

Domesticity is a life-long commitment with eternal benefits. By God's grace and the teaching of the older women in my life, I trust that He will enable me to accomplish all that He has set before me. My challenge to all young women is. . . Come home and change the world!

CHAPTER THREE

Queen of the Home

A virtuous woman is a crown to her husband...
(Proverbs 12:4)

Nothing is more beautiful than when a woman is a crown to her husband . . . an extension of all that he is. When a wife embraces this vision of her role, the rewards are a man who will conquer the world for her.

—Kelly Crawford

He that is blessed with a good wife is as happy as if he were upon the throne, for she is no less than a crown to him. A virtuous woman, that is pious and prudent, ingenious and industrious, that is active for the good of her family and looks well to the ways of her household, that makes conscience of her duty in every relation, a woman of spirit, that can bear crosses without disturbance, such a one owns her husband for her head, and therefore she is a crown to him, not only a credit and honour to him, as a crown is an ornament, but supports and keeps up his authority in his family, as a crown is an ensign of power. She is submissive and faithful to him, and by her example teaches his children and servants to be so too.

—*Matthew Henry*
Matthew Henry's Commentary on the Whole Bible:
Complete and Unabridged in One Volume

You Are a Crown
by Nancy Campbell

Where do you fit with your husband? You may have read the famous quote of Matthew Henry on the creation of the woman, "The woman was made of a rib out of the side of Adam, not made out of his head to rule over him, nor out of his feet to be trampled upon by him, but out of his side to be equal with him, under his arm to be protected, and near his heart to be beloved."

The Word of God also tells us in 1 Corinthians 11:7 that the "woman is the glory of the man." As the glory of the man, she is also a crown to honor her husband.

Proverbs 12:4 says, "A virtuous woman is a crown to her husband: but she that maketh ashamed is as rottenness in his bones." I love the Amplified version which says, "A virtuous and worthy wife—earnest and strong in character—is a crowning joy to her husband."

Isn't it interesting that God says a virtuous woman is a crown? She is not to be trodden underfoot. She is not to be looked down upon. She is not inferior. She is a crown. A crown is worn upon the head. A crown is something that is dazzlingly beautiful. It is usually made of gold and ornamented with precious gems. It is a token of honor.

Noah Webster's 1928 dictionary says: "'To crown' means to invest with royalty. To bestow something upon as a mark of honor or dignity; to adorn, dignify; also to award first rank."

Point five of 'to crown' In Webster's says, "Anything which imparts beauty, splendor, honor or finish; also the highest state or quality of anything." And on this point he quotes Proverbs 12:4.

A virtuous woman adds distinction and dignity to her husband. He is proud to wear her. He wants to show her off. He praises her before others.

When she honors him as king of her home, he will rise to kingly heights in his manhood. When she awards him 'first rank' he becomes free to reach his full potential and is inspired to do things he never thought possible. He will treat his wife like a Queen with dignity and respect.

Have you crowned your husband? The more richly you crown him, the more you will be blessed.

What does the crown look like with which you adorn your husband? Does it look tarnished and strange because many jewels are missing? Or is it filled with precious gems? What are some of the gems that will make your husband proud to wear you as his crown?

Is your crown decorated with diamonds of devotion, dedication, dignity, and diligence that will delight his soul?

Have you set in sapphires that will shine and sparkle with a serving, sacrificial and submissive spirit? Are you sweet to him? Are you a strength and support to his vision and goals in life? Are you sensitive to his needs? Are you steadfast in your loyalty and commitment to your marriage?

Have you positioned pearls in your crown—pearls of patience, peace, perseverance and prayer for your husband?

Oh don't forget the rubies, the rarest of all gems. Is your crown radiating with rubies of reverence and respect for your husband?

Is your crown ornamented with opals of openness, obedience, overflowing love and the oil of joy?

Don't forget the emeralds that emanate esteem, earnest commitment, encouragement and endurance.

Adorn your crown with amethysts of admiration, affection, affirmation, approval, appreciation and attentiveness.

Just a minute! You can't forget the crowning jewel of all—contentment! This jewel adds luster to your crown. This jewel releases your husband from bondage and pressure. Sadly, it is often a missing jewel. It's easy to be content when you have everything you want. But can you learn to be content when you don't have everything you want? Can you be content with what your husband provides for you? I am always challenged by Psalm 128:3 TLB where it talks about the "contented" wife in the home.

"If I do all this, he'll walk all over me," you say. "He'll become proud and he's already got a big enough head!" It doesn't work that way, dear one. When you forget about yourself and seek to bless and serve your husband, you not only crown him with dignity and honor, but you truly become his crown. You won't be subservient. You'll be worn on his head as his most treasured possession.

Why not start adding precious jewels to your crown today?

If I were a Queen,
What would I do?
I'd make you King,
And I'd wait on you.

Christina Rossetti

Our homes are also the frame for a very special picture that has been entrusted to Christian husbands and wives. Paul wrote that marriage is meant to be a picture of Christ and His Heavenly Bride, the Church. Our homes set the stage for this picture and how it is presented to our world. Does your home reflect a wholehearted devotion to its King—your husbands and fathers? Does your home show a tender love and care for its Queen—all of you wives, mothers, and grandmothers? Your home can either lie about Christ and His Bride, or it can tell the truth. The truth is that the King provides for His Bride, lays down His life for her, and honors her with His own Body. The truth is that the Bride adores the King, delights in serving Him, and rejoices at His return.

—*Jennie Chancey*

"What do you think the beautiful word 'wife' comes from?" he asks. "It means 'weaver.'" You must either be house-wives or house-moths; remember that. In the deep sense, you must weave men's fortunes, and embroider them, or feed upon them, and bring them to decay. Wherever a true wife comes, home is always around her. The stars may be the canopy over her head, the glow-worm in the night's cold grass be the fire at her feet, but home is where she is; and for a noble woman it stretches far around her—better than houses with ceilings of cedar, or with paintings of the masters, shedding its quiet light for those who else were homeless.

—*John Ruskin*

The Noble Wife

by J.R. Miller, excerpted from *The Family*, 1882

It is a high honor for a woman to be chosen from among all womankind to be the wife of a good and true man. She is lifted up to be a crowned queen. Her husband's manly love laid at her feet exalts her to the throne of his life. Great power is placed in her hands. Sacred destinies are reposed in her keeping. Will she wear her crown beneficently? Will she fill her realm with beauty and with blessing? Or will she fail in her holy trust? Only her married life can be the answer.

A true wife makes a man's life nobler, stronger, grander, by the omnipotence of her love "turning all the forces of manhood upward and heavenward." While she clings to him in holy confidence and loving dependence, she brings out in him whatever is noblest and richest in his being. She inspires him with courage and earnestness. She beautifies his life. She softens whatever is rude and harsh in his habits or his spirit. She clothes him with the gentler graces of refined and cultured manhood. While she yields to him and never disregards his lightest wish, she is really his queen, ruling his whole life and leading him onward and upward in every proper path.

Again, let me say that no wife can over estimate the influence she wields over her husband or the measure in which his character, his career and his very destiny are laid in her hands for shaping. The sway which she holds over him is the sway of love, but it is mighty and resistless. If she retains her power, if she holds her place as queen of his life, she can do with him as she will. Even unconsciously to herself, without any thought of her responsibility, she will exert over him an influence that will go far toward making or marring all his future. If she has no lofty conception of life herself, if she is vain and frivolous, she will only chill his ardor, weaken his resolution and draw him aside from any earnest endeavor.

But if she has in her soul noble womanly qualities, if she has true thoughts of life, if she has purpose, strength of character and fidelity to principle, she will be to him an unfailing inspiration toward all that is noble, manly and Christlike. The high conceptions of life in her mind will elevate his conceptions. Her firm, strong purpose will put vigor and determination into every resolve and act of his. Her purity of soul will cleanse and refine his spirit. Her warm interest in all his affairs and her wise counsel at every point will make him strong for every duty and valiant in every struggle. Her careful domestic management will become an important element of success in his business life. Her bright, orderly, happy homemaking will be a perpetual source of joy and peace, and an incentive to nobler living. Her unwavering fidelity, her tender affectionateness, her womanly sympathy, her beauty of soul, will make her to him God's angel indeed, sheltering, guarding, keeping, guiding, and blessing him. Just in the measure in which she realizes this lofty ideal of wifehood will she fulfill her mission and reap the rich harvest of her hopes.

Such is the "woman's lot" that falls on every wife. It is solemn enough to make her very thoughtful and very earnest. How can she make sure that her influence over her husband will be for good, that he will be a better man, more successful in his career and happier, because she is his wife? Not by any mere moral posturing so as to seem to have lofty purpose and wise thoughts of life; not by any weak resolving to help him and be an uplifting inspiration to him; not by perpetual preaching and lecturing on a husband's duties and on manly character; she can do it only by being in the very depths of her soul, in every thought and impulse of her heart and in every fiber of her nature, a true and noble woman. She will make him not like what she tells him he ought to be, but like what she herself is.

Called to Queenhood
by Nancy Campbell

There is a quality of queenliness in every woman. You innately desire it. Your husband desires it, and as king, he wants you to be his queen. We see it in our young daughters and granddaughters. They want to be princesses. They want to dress up as princesses when they play 'dress ups; they are subconsciously practicing to be queens. They love to play 'mommies and daddies' with their dolls; they are intuitively preparing for motherhood. We don't teach them to do this. They do it naturally . . . until their minds are re-programmed by the humanistic propaganda of our modern society.

Just as men should walk in kingliness, so we should walk in queenliness. And we have a queendom to reign over. Yes, there is such a word in the dictionary. Unfortunately it has become a forgotten word as women have left the glory of their homes to pursue vain callings, careers that may seem glamorous and enticing now, but which will one day be left behind. On the other hand, mothering, embracing and training children, and reigning over a queendom will powerfully affect the nation, the generations to come and even more powerfully, eternity!

You may live in a 10,000-square-foot home or you may live in a humble trailer. No matter how big and palatial, or how small and humble your home, you are still queen of your castle. Our daughter, Evangeline and her husband, live in a two-roomed cabin with their eight children. Is she groveling with self-pity and acting like a non-entity? No, she is queen of her domain. She lives likes a queen. She thinks like a queen. She runs her home with amazing efficiency. There is no mess, no confusion, no extra 'stuff' and no complaining— only joy, fun, positivity, and a family living in the presence of the Lord. Many times when the three sisters get together, they have great confabulations on how they can better organize their homes and live in a more queenly way.

One of the meanings of queen in the dictionary is "a woman who is eminent or supreme in a given domain." That's us, ladies! God has given us a domain to rule and reign over as queens. Where is this domain? It is not the realm of the corporate world. It is not ruling over our husbands. We are privileged to submit to our husband's leadership, authority, and protection. However, under his covering and protection, God has given us a sphere of rulership—a realm where we are to rule and reign! This realm is in our homes.

"Oh, how boring!" I hear you exclaim. Wait a minute. This is the very reason that many women have lost their queenliness today. They have been brainwashed into thinking that the home is a boring place, a place where they will lose their identity and amount to nothing. The very opposite is the truth. The home is where we find our identity. In the safety and sanctity of the home, we can flourish to our full beauty. We can give vent to our creativity. We can fulfill our management abilities.

The Old Testament calls us "the mistress of the house." One Hebrew word for "mistress" is *baalah*, which is simply the feminine word for *baal*. It means 'to be master, to have dominion over.' The other word for "mistress" in the Old Testament is the Hebrew word *gbereth*. It is the feminine word of master, *gbiyr*, and means "to be strong, valiant, to prevail."

It is not only men who want to have dominion. There is something in a woman that also wants to have dominion too. God created us this way. Immediately after God told Adam and Eve to "Be fruitful, and multiply, and replenish the earth." He then said to them, "Subdue it, and have dominion." These words were not only spoken to the man, but also to the woman.

God wants you to be the mistress, the queen—governing over the domestic affairs of your home. Your home is the center of your life. It is a place of challenge, creativity, and celebration. You rule over your kitchen, making sure that your husband and family are daily nourished with life-giving meals. You preside over the educating of your children. You administrate the cleaning of your home. You direct the ideas, the projects, and the plans that you and your children are currently working on.

You practice hospitality—planning when you will invite each particular family or lonely person to come and eat at your table. You think about what food you will prepare for them and how you can make them feel special. You work on assignments with your children for reaching out to the poor and needy. You are constantly making your home a creative, interesting, and sacred place to live in.

You plan, plant, and work in your garden to feed your family and beautify your home. And above all, you are full-time nurturing, nourishing, loving and encouraging your husband and children. Oh your life is full! There is so much to reign over. You never seem to have enough time to fulfill all your great visions.

Of course, as queen of your home, you don't do everything yourself, but train your children to take over in all these areas. And you may have many servants— your washing machine, dryer, dishwasher and all your electric kitchen gadgets. What a blessing.

But is this only an Old Testament truth? Let's see what the New Testament has to say. 1 Timothy 5:14 says, "I will therefore that the younger women marry, bear children, guide the house, give none occasion to the adversary to speak reproachfully." The phrase, 'guide the house' is the Greek word *oikodespoteō*. It is a combination of two words—*oikos* meaning "home, household, family" and *despotes* meaning "master, or ruler."

What does this mean? You are the ruler, the queen of your queendom. It does not mean that you manage your husband's life. Your mandate is to manage and take dominion over the domestic affairs of your household and garden. God gives you the responsibility to manage your home and keep it in order.

Don't look at all the other things that you could be doing outside your home. Instead, look to the things that need to be taken care of in your home today. There's a lot to do. Is the laundry up-to-date? Are the dishes washed? Is your home running smoothly? Are you watching over the minds and hearts of your children? Are you watching in prayer?

I love the words of Rev. T. DeWitt Talmage:

Thank God, O woman, for the quietude of your home, and that you are queen in it. Men come at eventide to the home; but all day long you are there, beautifying it, sanctifying it, adorning it, blessing it. . . . It may be a very humble home. There may be no carpet on the floor. There may be no pictures on the wall. There may be no silks in the wardrobe; but, by your faith in God, and your cheerful demeanor, you may garniture that place with more splendor than the upholsterer's hand ever kindled.

God wants His kingdom to spread throughout the earth. He wants His glory, His love, His truth, His peace, and His salvation to touch all people. As we take dominion over our homes, as we make them sanctuaries for training godly children and palaces for God's glory, we will see God's kingdom spread.

Sadly, many women are bored with their home. They have not yet seen the vision that their home is their greatest sphere of influence for God. They do not have the vision for raising children for God. With no vision for hospitality and so little to rule over, they are unfulfilled and have to find their place of dominion somewhere else. Unfortunately, they move out of the sphere where God wants them to govern. They come out from under their husband's protection and become vulnerable to other men instead of their own husband. As one writer commented, "Women end up submitting to many men in the corporate world because they refuse to submit to one man at home." The result is an epidemic of divorce and breakdown of marriage, even in the Christian world. Isn't it sad that current statistics reveal that the emptiest place in America during the day is the home?

The Queen of England has a number of castles. The people know which one she is visiting or residing in when they see the flag flown at the top of the castle. Fly the flag at your royal home. Don't vacate your queendom for a lesser career.

"But I don't feel like a queen," you answer. It is not a matter of feelings. It is who you are. Rise up to your status of queenship. Think like a queen and you will begin to act like a queen. Walk like a queen. Speak like a queen—this will definitely make you feel more queenly. It will also change the atmosphere in your home. It will draw praises from your husband. What about dressing like a queen? You will rise to how you dress.

The more you live like a queen, the more honor you will give to your husband and the more he will be motivated to walk in his kingliness. Proverbs 12:4 says that a virtuous woman is a crown to her husband. A crown is a symbol of royalty. A crown is beautiful, adorned with shining and valuable gems. As we take on our queenship, we will be a crown to our husbands.

Woman's Mission

When the husbandman grows weary,
And the heart is full with strife,
And the skies so sad and dreary,
With their darkness shadow life;
Then comes the noble woman,

With her hands so true and kind;
With her heart divinely human,
All his troublous griefs to bind.

Silently her presence showers,
Sunshine calm in noble deed,
Clothing with new hopes and powers,
All of who her help have need;
Toils may her kind words soften,
Countless are her deeds of good;
Winning her a pray'r most often,
For her noble womanhood.

Rebecca Darr
"Grange Melodies" Songbook, 1891

The True Wife's Kingdom

by J.R. Miller, excerpted from *Secrets of Happy Home Life*, 1874

Home is the true wife's kingdom. There, first of all places, she must be strong and beautiful. She may touch life outside in many ways, if she can do it without slighting the duties that are hers within her own doors. But if any calls for her service must be declined, they should not be the duties of her home. These are hers, and no other one's. Very largely does the wife hold in her hands, as a sacred trust, the happiness and the highest good of the hearts that nestle there. The best husband—

the truest, the noblest, the gentlest, the richest-hearted—cannot make his home happy if his wife be not, in every reasonable sense, a helpmate to him.

In the last analysis, home happiness depends on the wife. Her spirit gives the home its atmosphere. Her hands fashion its beauty. Her heart makes its love. And the end is so worthy, so noble, so divine, that no woman who has been called to be a wife, and has listened to the call, should consider any price too great to pay, to be the light, the joy, the blessing, the inspiration of a home.

Men with fine gifts think it worth while to live to paint a few great pictures which shall be looked at and admired for generations; or to write a few songs which shall sing themselves into the ears and hearts of men. But the woman who makes a sweet, beautiful home, filling it with love and prayer and purity, is doing something better than anything else her hands could find to do beneath the skies.

CHAPTER FOUR

The Monarch of the Cradle

Look for one single moment upon the power of the cradle, for all this love was not meant to be expended merely as a luxury for the maternal bosom—there is meaning in it. It is one of the sources of the greatest power that exists on earth. The power of the cradle is greater than the power of the throne, greater than royalty in its diffusion and in its capacity of usefulness— ten thousand times greater. Make me monarch of the cradles, and I will give to whosoever will the monarchy of the kingdoms and of the throne.

—Beecher

You see, there is no higher calling, no greater privilege than being a vessel of life and later a teacher of souls which will live for ever. This is a crucial point: These children will live forever, either in Heaven, or in Hell. We not only have the privilege of introducing them to the world, but God has given us the honor of assisting our husbands in the great work of introducing these little ones to the God Who loves them. No empire, no credential, no golden treasure, no corporate success story can ever rival the glory of this calling.

Praying mothers, teaching mothers, faithful mothers—the Church needs you. She needs mothers who will crave children, and love them and bless them to be the warriors of the next generation.

Motherhood! Blessed motherhood! The time has come to once again sing the praises of this calling. Though bloodied by the barbs of feminism, Christian motherhood will not be vanquished.

—*Beall Phillips,* Verses of Virtue

The Cost of Motherhood
by Douglas Phillips

Once a lady went to visit her friend. During the visit, the children of the friend entered the room and began to play with each other. As the lady and her friend visited, the lady turned to her friend and said eagerly and yet with evidently no thought of the meaning of her words: "Oh, I'd give my life to have such children." The mother replied with a subdued earnestness whose quiet told of the depth of experience out of which her words came: "That's exactly what it costs."

There is a cost of motherhood. And the price is no small sum. And if you are not willing to pay this price, no amount of encouragement about the joys of motherhood will satisfy.

But the price of motherhood is not fundamentally different from the price of being a disciple of Jesus Christ. In fact, Christian mothers see their duty as mothers flowing from their calling to Jesus Christ. And what is this cost?

Christian motherhood means dedicating your entire life in service of others. It means standing beside your husband, following him, and investing in the lives of children whom you hope will both survive you and surpass you. It means forgoing present satisfaction for eternal rewards. It means investing in the lives of others who may never fully appreciate your sacrifice or comprehend the depth of your love. And it means doing all these things, not because you will receive the praise of man—for you will not—but because God made you to be a woman and a mother, and there is great contentment in that biblical calling.

In other words, Motherhood requires vision. It requires living by faith and not by sight.

These are some of the reasons why Motherhood is both the most biblically noble and the most socially unappreciated role to which a young woman can aspire. There are many people who ask the question: Does my life matter? But a mother that fears the Lord need never ask such a question. Upon her faithful obedience hinges the future of the church and the hope of the nation.

Oh, that God would give every mother a vision of the glory and splendor of the work that is given to her when a babe is placed in her bosom to be nursed and trained! Could she have but one glimpse into the future of that life as it reaches on into eternity; could she be made to understand her own personal responsibility for the training of this child, for the development of its life, and for its destiny—she would see that in all God's world there is no other work so noble and so worthy of her best powers, and she would commit to no other hands the sacred and holy trust give to her.

—*J.R. Miller,* The Family

To marry and have children is the ideal life for a woman. What career could ever be as fine? To give the world splendid men and women—isn't that the noblest thing a woman could possibly do?

—*Jessie Willcox Smith*

Yes, my oldest daughter has a big responsibility in helping care for our family. But here's the difference: In our family, we verbally and physically exalt the blessing of children. Regardless of the diapers, the messes and the squabbles, we view this work as the most noble on earth. She understands that this work goes far beyond the physical demands; that no woman could hold greater power than that of helping shape an immortal life.

—*Kelly Crawford*

The Majesty of Motherhood
by Karen Andreola

Day of Coronation

A less-talked-about detail about the godly woman is tucked away in Proverbs 31. Here we learn that her clothing is of fine linen and she actually wears the color purple. For centuries this once hard-to-come-by and expensive fabric dye has been associated with royalty. And it is this rich color that belongs to the godly homemaker.

Purple is representative of the majesty of motherhood; it represents her high calling. Dear mother, you are the queen of your household. The day your first baby was placed in your arms was your coronation day. Yes, while you were gazing into the face of your precious one, a little one so fresh from heaven, you were crowned queen. You were crowned with authority by the Almighty God.

Authority in the Home Atmosphere

There is a "temptation of ease" in the household when a weary mother is ever so much with her children. That temptation is to be "buddy-buddy" or "palsy-walsy" in too many circumstances. In this case, Mother may succumb to the whims, wants, and whines of her children as the presence of her authority dwindles or fades away, blending into the background kitchen wallpaper. One good fruit of home education is the close relationship that develops between mother and child. It is valuable and necessary for a loving, warm, home atmosphere. Rules only, without relationship, invite rebellion. But let's look at the flip side. Relationship only, without rules (to be obeyed, promptly and without complaint) promotes disorder and friction. A child's regular outspoken, soft-spoken or unspoken, "But I don't want to . . ." is a symptom of a household that is democratic.

While reading the remarkable writings of the Victorian Christian and British educator, Miss Charlotte

Mason, I came to see more clearly that a very different form of government is to be established in the home. The government of the family is to be an absolute monarchy. The domestic rulers are precisely as follows: Father is king and Mother is queen.

To Serve and Be Served, To Love and Be Loved

At the time of the year 2000 celebrations a vast majority of people voted Queen Elizabeth I of England a favorite person of the millennium. I happened to be reading aloud to my children from Queen Elizabeth and the Spanish Armada by Frances Winwar. When I got to the following sentences, I jotted them down. "It is not easy to be queen. But she was a queen, and so always she must think first for her country and her people, before she thought of herself." Isn't this what a loving and diligent mother does everyday as she serves the children of her realm in all the hundreds of little duties she carries out minute by minute, hour by hour, day by day?

Children also have a part to play in this mini-kingdom of the home. A good queen expects her subjects to, in turn, faithfully serve her. Because Miss Charlotte Mason was a British educator it seems apropos that she would be better familiar with the characteristics of royalty from her country's heritage. She said, "It is good for the children to faithfully serve, honor, and humbly obey their natural rulers. Only at home can children be trained in the chivalrous temper of proud submission and dignified obedience; and if the parents do not inspire and foster deference, reverence, and loyalty, how shall these crowning graces of character thrive in a hard and emulous world?"

Mothers Are to Reflect the Majesty of God

The chief business of the parent is to be an inspirer. And Mother must reflect the majesty of God. Charlotte Mason says, "We have not only to fulfill His counsels regarding children, but to represent His Person. We parents are as God to the little child; and yet a more constraining thought, God is to him what his parents are; he has not power to conceive a greater and lovelier personality than that of the royal heads of his home; he makes his first approach to the Infinite through them."

In our present American secular society, it seems too many parents have abdicated the throne. Mothers have left the home, their place of ladyship and leadership, because they can find little value, and thus little satisfaction, in homemaking or home teaching. Passively parents allow others (experts or institutions or peers) to have a stronger influence on their children—a stronger influence than home. Yet parents have been given a charge to train up their children, and there is a remnant of those who reign. They understand that it is not an option to either lay aside or to sink under the burden of the honor God has laid upon them.

A Strong Home Influences Society

Mothers who recognize the value of homemaking see that there is an art to it. A mother builds a happy home brick by brick, laid upon strong moral principles. From her home the majesty of her inspiring leadership has a spiral affect. Like a pebble dropped in a pond, it spirals outward in ever widening circles. Rather than society influencing the home, it ought to be the Christian home influencing society. Righteousness brings beauty of character. Character creates harmony in the home. Harmony in the home fosters order to civilization. This is what makes peace on earth. Isn't this what is meant by "the hand that rocks the cradle rules the world?"

Therefore, let us remember our position, fulfilling our office of queen with a kind of friendly dignity. It is a noble, high, important and sometimes difficult position—"uneasy lies the head that wears a crown," even if it is the natural crown of motherhood. But God will guide our steps if we keep our eyes on He who appointed us. And we will find joy within the authoritative yet loving relationship we were meant to establish with our children.

The mother in her office, holds the key
Of the soul; and she it is who stamps the coin
Of character, and makes the being who would be a savage

But for her gentle cares, a Christian man;
Then crown her queen of the world.

Author Unknown

No artist's work is so high, so noble, so grand so enduring, so important for all time, as the making of character in a child.

—*Charlotte Cushman*

Reclaiming the Lost Vision of Motherhood
by June Fuentes

O' for mothers to hold in their hands a child whose soul is eternal and to grasp the vision of changing the world through her mothering as she purposes toward multigenerational faithfulness.

To look into the eyes of her child and know that God has put a purpose for that child here on earth—to advance the kingdom of heaven—which is glorifying the Father he serves above. Mothers are also put on earth for royal purposes, to raise children for the King. Shaping and molding them to one day become warriors for the Lord.

Mothers, do we understand that what is done in the

four walls of our home— that it is holy work done to the Lord? As we teach that small child to stand, are you praying that one day he will stand strong for the Lord against wickedness? As you teach him to walk, are you teaching them to walk to the lost and preach the gospel? When you teach them to read, are you telling them that one day they will read the Word to the masses and that lives will be transformed forever?

In other words, are you raising your children to be world changers? Yesterday I gathered all my children together and shared with them how God gave them life for the soul purpose of changing the world—for Him. Who is the child who understands his purpose in life— his calling? Where is the child who has been whispered to and reminded that he will one day change the world since he was a wee babe? How would our lives have been different had our mothers embraced such a vision?

As mothers, we need to equip our children well to do the work the Lord has assigned for them to do. We must diligently teach Scripture, we must teach godly character, we must teach love for the Lord and the lost without growing discouraged ourselves for we have the Master's work at hand, an honorable and momentous responsibility! We must understand that lost souls could be at stake and nations could be destroyed if we do not fulfill this high calling of motherhood. We cannot simply render ourselves weary and ultimately give up.

Do you notice that little boy who is playing in the sandbox? He might very well be the world's next church planter. That little girl in the corner who is quietly playing dolls might one day raise a martyr for Christ. The little baby in your arms whom you cradle today could very well go to Africa one day and share the gospel to the lost tribes.

I am convinced that the greatest world changers have not been written about in history books, and that only God knows who they are. They are God's best kept secrets. They are the unnoticed people in society. They are the ones who do great and mighty works in private where only He sees. They are the ones that make a difference through the one small, powerful act that the Lord assigned them. These will be richly rewarded in Heaven for their faithfulness.

Our lasting influence impacts future generations through our children, our grandchildren and great grandchildren, whether for good or for evil. Which are you raising for the Lord? Descendants who could be an army to take the world by storm or descendants who build up altars to false gods? We must revive the vision of multigenerational faithfulness! We cannot change our homes through the efforts of our flesh — it comes from grace and power from God alone—but we are required to do our part. We cannot fall short of this glorious vocation because our Lord has called us to it. And what He calls us to we must obey.

Now, in honor those great mothers who have come

before us who have sacrificed their lives, gave unselfishly, wept in the dark to the Savior and persevered to the end— we applaud you! You have paved the way for us behind you! The Lord has used you as a mighty instrument in His hand, and you are surely called blessed among your children. Your dedication has lasting power that is the sweet aroma of Jesus Christ.

God certainly uses the weak to shame the strong. And he uses ordinary people who serve an amazing God that has extraordinary plans to help us reclaim our vision for motherhood and build a godly nation for Him.

Rich, Though Poor

Come gather round me, merry ones,
And here as I sit down,
With shouts of laughter on me place
A mimic regal crown.
Say, mighty king, would I accept
Your armies and domain,
Or e'en your crown, and never feel
These little hands again?

There's more of honor in their touch,
And blessing unto me,
Than kingdom unto kingdom joined,

Or navies on the sea;
So greater gifts by them are brought
Than Sheba's queen did bring
To him who at Jerusalem
Was born to be a king.

A.D.F. Randolph

You are in the very center of His will as you embrace His little ones to your heart and raise them to be mighty arrows for God's kingdom. You are at the very heart of the kingdom of God. There is nothing more powerful that you could be doing in the whole of the world. Be encouraged. And may you be filled with the joy of the Lord as you fulfill this mighty task in your home today.

—*Nancy Campbell*

Who is the Queen of Baby Land?
Mother kind and sweet,
And her love, born above,
Guides the little feet.

Author Unknown

The nursery is the department of home in which the mother fulfills her peculiar mission. This is her special sphere. None can effectually take her place there. She is the center of attraction, the guardian of the infant's destiny; and none like she, can overrule the unfolding life and character of the child. God has fitted her for the work of the nursery. Here she reigns supreme, the arbitress of the everlasting weal or woe of untutored infancy. On her the fairest hopes of educated man depend, and in the exercise of her power there, she sways a nation's destiny, gives to the infant body and soul their beauty, their bias and their direction. She there possesses the immense force of first impressions. The soul of her child lies unveiled before her, and she makes the stamp of her own spirit and personality upon its pliable nature. She there engrafts it, as it were, into her own being, and from the combined elements of her own character, builds up and establishes the character of her offspring. Hers will, therefore, be the glory or the shame.

—*Samuel Phillips,* The Christian Home, *1865*

She Always Made Home Happy

In an old church-yard stood a stone
Weather-marked and stained;
The hand of time had crumbled it,

So only part remained.
Upon one side I could just trace
"In memory of our mother";
An epitaph which spoke of home
Was chiseled on the other.

I've gazed on monuments of fame,
High towering to the skies;
I've seen the sculptured marble stone
Where a great hero lies;
But by this epitaph I paused
And read it o'er and o'er,
For I had never seen inscribed
Such words as these before.

"She always made home happy." What
A noble record left;
A legacy of memory sweet
To those she loved bereft;
And what a testimony given
By those who knew her best,
Engraven on this plain rude stone
That marked their mother's rest.

So then was stilled her weary heart,
Folded her hands so white,
And she was carried from the home
She'd always made so bright.
Her children raised a monument
That money could not buy,

As witness of a noble life,
Whose record is on high.

A noble life, but written not
In any book of fame;
Among the list of noted ones
None ever saw her name;
For only her own household knew
The victories she had won,
And none but they could testify
How well her work was done.

Author Unknown

Noble Mothers in Sacred Homes
by June Fuentes

Mothers of the past have had the great honor of keeping the world at bay by creating a magnificently glorious haven within the home. It was a fortress of refuge, a place of solitude, a holy shelter of rest against a perverse world that would be happy to consume her beloved family members. Her spirit lives among us today among mothers possessing gentle and quiet resolve, her determined love making a difference in every life she touches. These noble mothers found great satisfaction creatively weaving homes that embraced, encouraged, and rejuvenated their loved ones at the end of the day. But today's mother unfortunately struggles immensely just understanding who they are and just what motherhood is because, through the course of history, the lines have been subtly and deceptively blurred:

> *Women sigh for fame. They would be sculptors, and chisel out of the cold stone forms of beauty to fill the world with admiration of their skill. Or they would be poets, to write songs to thrill a nation and to be sung around the world. But is any work in marble so great as her who has an immortal life laid in her hands to shape for its destiny?*

> —J.R. Miller

Women today need to be taught the true meaning and behold the vision of what biblical motherhood stands for. There is nothing more breathtakingly beautiful than a mother that truly loves the Lord, passionately embraces her family and home and understands her noble and blessed purpose on earth.

This mother does not allow the world to steal away from her what she has been uniquely made for and she rejects the world's misleading definition of what motherhood looks like—high power career, colossal home, newest car, perfect children. The infamous misleading notion of being able to have it all, but never divulging the high price that must be paid.

And truth be told, she already has it all. And the wise mother knows it, whether she is young or old, rich or poor, and her heart is happy and simply content.

A Work Like No Other
Author Unknown, c. 1893

The mother's work is unlike any other in the whole world. It entails the constant drawing out of the very depths of her nature, and keeps it on the stretch often for hours together. It is from morning till night, and often does not end with night.

But different calls are made on her at different times; that is where the difficulty and the need of adaptation arise. She must, like a musician on a rich toned organ, frequently at a moment's notice, pull out a new stop and push in all the others—thus only can she supply the harmony of family life. She must be ready to meet these sudden, rapid changes, these calls on her love and her sympathy on all sides. She must go from the anxiety of a sick room to a cheerful meal, without casting sorrow around her; from the practical and troublesome study of economies to join the intellectual joys which have no price on earth. She may come in from visits to her poorer neighbours, and while her heart aches at leaving some terrible sight, she must at once devote her whole attention to something her children have been waiting for, the rehearsal of a play, perhaps, in which they cannot do without her, and in which all her best powers must be used.

In these rapid changes, she must shew no dismay, no surprise; they are her life. She must reckon herself as rightly the servant of all while she is the mistress of all, and must take the smallest details as not only "all in the day's work," but as her own special province and one of her joys in life, as that about which it warms her heart to think that she, and she alone, is the one who can in the end order and arrange them for the comfort and well-being of the little community under her charge.

In order to succeed in this, she must bring all her powers to bear on it with definite intention, just as the skillful musician would. Details, interruptions, perplexities, all must be, as it were, part of one great whole, must minister to the efficiency of the one great work, the fulfillment of the one ideal. This ideal is the same for the woman of high rank, with her large household and her heavy social responsibilities, as for the quiet "home-maker" who has but one little maid of-all-work to direct. Both alike have husband and children to care for, and of the two the second has perhaps the making of her own life most entirely in her own hands. To be Queen over her little kingdom, serene in every family emergency, capable to direct all things with calmness, cheerfulness, and decision, is an ambition sufficient to tax the powers of the most skillful amongst us, and a vocation equal to the highest God has appointed on this earth.

Ideals of Life

You may talk of fashion's leader—
Paint her finer than a queen,
And try to make our lowly lot
And lowly living mean;
But I tell you, sir, the fairest
And the best that I have seen,

Were common men and women,
Used to humble work and ways;
Doing what was right and honest
Without favor, without praise,
Lighting up the night behind them
With the brightness of their days.

There is one that shines upon me
From the mists of memory—
A woman with the weakness
Of a woman, it may be;—
And naught to me are social queens
While earth holds such as she!

Her homespun sleeve is more to me
Than all your bordered trains;
For in the blessed realm of love
She sweetly rules and reigns.

You may follow fashion's fancy
But I pray you, have the grace
To leave the little, homely house,
And flowery garden-place,
And the window with the sunshine
Of this dear, remembered face!

You may follow fashion's fancy
But I pray you, leave to me
The chair there in the corner,
Just the way it used to be,
And the dear devoted mother,
With her children at her knee.

Author Unknown

A true mother is one of the holiest secrets of home happiness. God sends many beautiful things to this world, many noble gifts; but no blessing is richer than that which He bestows in a mother who has learned love's lessons well, and has realized something of the meaning of her sacred calling.

—*J.R. Miller,* Secrets of Happy Home Life

A woman is seen in her most sacred and dignified character as wife and mother. She has great influence over the character of individuals, over the condition of families, and over the destinies of empires.

It is a fact that many of the noblest patriots, our most profound scholars, and our holiest ministers, were stimulated to their excellence and usefulness by those holy principles which they derived in early years from devoted mothers

...our mothers are our earliest instructors, and they have an influence over us, the importance of which, for time and eternity, surpasses the power of language to describe.

—*Daughters of Destiny*

The Hand That Rocks the Cradle

Blessings on the hand of women!
Angels guard its strength and grace,
In the palace, cottage, hovel,
Oh, no matter where the place;
Would that never storms assailed it,
Rainbows ever gently curled;
For the hand that rocks the cradle
Is the hand that rules the world.

Infancy's the tender fountain,
Power may with beauty flow,
Mother's first to guide the streamlets,
From them souls unresting grow—
Grow on for the good or evil,
Sunshine streamed or evil hurled;
For the hand that rocks the cradle
Is the hand that rules the world.

Woman, how divine your mission
Here upon our natal sod!
Keep, oh, keep the young heart open
Always to the breath of God!
All true trophies of the ages
Are from mother-love impearled;
For the hand that rocks the cradle
Is the hand that rules the world.

Blessings on the hand of women!
Fathers, sons, and daughters cry,
And the sacred song is mingled
With the worship in the sky—
Mingles where no tempest darkens,
Rainbows evermore are hurled;
For the hand that rocks the cradle
Is the hand that rules the world.

William Ross Wallace

To be a mother is the grandest vocation in the world. No one being has a position of such power and influence. She holds in her hands the destiny of nations; for to her is necessarily committed the making of the nation's citizens.

—Hannah Whitall Smith

You may place upon the brow of a true wife and mother the greenest laurels; you may crowd her hands with civic honors; but, after all, to her there will be no place like home, and the crown of her motherhood will be more precious than the diadem of a queen.

—Francis E. W. Harper, Enlightened Motherhood

For a Christian, having babies is not about birthing pains, changing diapers or baking cookies (though it includes all of these). Having babies is about transforming the world forever. This investment will last, not for thirty years, not for my lifetime, but f-o-r-e-v-e-r. The investment is realized on earth and pays dividends for eternity. On earth, we pray that these children will advance the very kingdom of God. But in heaven, the souls of every redeemed child will stand with me throughout eternity before the Lord Jesus. The pressures of today (be they financial, physical, etc.) that taunt Christians to self-consciously distort God's fruitful purpose for the womb, and to separate life from love, will seem infinitesimally small as we look back upon this whisper of a life with our children beside us in eternity.

My children can have more far-reaching implications for society and posterity than anything else I can do. Having babies and training children for Jesus Christ means my life work will last forever. I refuse to accept the minimizing, selfish, materialistic, and limited vision of womanhood dispensed by the apostles of modernity and relevancy in this generation. My dream is far greater.

—*Beall Phillips*

They brought up their families in sturdy virtue and a living faith in God without which nations perish.

—*Inscription on the Pilgrim Mother's Monument in Plymouth, MA*

True Artists
by Robert Lewis Dabney

Your task is unobtrusive; it is performed in the privacy of home, and by the gentle touches of daily love. But it is the noblest work which mortal can perform for it furnishes the polished stones (godly children), with which the temple of our liberties must be repaired. We have seen men building a lofty pile of sculptured marble, where columns with polished shafts pointed to the skies, and domes reared their arches on high, like mimic heavens. They swung the massive blocks into their places on the walls with cranes and cables, with shout and outcries, and hugh creaking of the ponderous machinery. But these were not the true artisans: they were but labourers.

The true artists, whose priceless cunning was to give immortal beauty to the pile, and teach the dead stones to breathe majesty and grace were not there. None saw or heard their labours. In distant and quiet workrooms, where no eye watched them, and no shout gave signal of their motions, they plied their patient chisels slowly with gentle touches, evoking the forms of beauty which lay hid in the blocks before them.

Such is your work; the home and fireside are the scenes of your industry. But the materials which you shape are the souls of men, which are to compose the fabric of our church and state. The politician, the professional man, is but the day labourer, who moves and lifts the finished block to its place. You are the true artists, who endue it with fitness and beauty; and therefore yours is the nobler task.

Oh, Mothers of young children, I bow before you in reverence. Your work is most holy. You are fashioning the destinies of immortal souls. The powers folded up in the little ones you hushed to sleep in your bosoms last night, are powers that shall exist for ever. You are preparing them for their immortal destiny and influence. Be faithful. Take up your sacred burden reverently...

—*J.R. Miller*

CHAPTER FIVE

The Power of Parenthood

It is not open to parents either to lay aside or to sink under the burden of the honour laid upon them; and, no doubt, we have all seen the fullest, freest flow of confidence, sympathy, and love between parent and child where the mother sits as a queen among her children and the father is honoured as a crowned head. The fact that there are two parents, each to lend honour to the other, yet free from restraint in each other's presence, makes it the easier to maintain the impalpable 'state' of parenthood. And the presence of the slight, sweet, undefined feeling of dignity in the household is the very first condition for the bringing-up of loyal, honourable men and women, capable of reverence and apt to win respect.

—*Charlotte Mason*, Parents and Children

Raising Noble Children
by Douglas Phillips

The call to Christian manhood and womanhood is a noble calling. It is a holy pursuit. It is a life-long duty of service that we must ever strive to carry out faithfully, and in the furtherance of this goal, it is important that we are mindful of Whom we are called to serve: Christ, our King. And as children of the King, we must hold His banner high without wavering. We must walk in a manner befitting those who bear the name of Him who is the "great King over all the earth" (Psalm 47:2).

This is a vision that our sons and daughters must understand from their youth. This is the vision parents are to cast for their children and incorporate into every area of life. As Harvey Newcomb wrote to sons, "What you are while you are a boy, you will be when you become a man." Our boys will only walk with noble purpose as Christ's vice-regents if they are trained to act the part of noble men. And so it is with our girls: they will only comport themselves as daughters of Zion if they are shown what this means in vivid and unmistakable terms.

As we train our children, we must direct their every endeavor in light of Christ's all-encompassing Kingship, even as the Psalmist recognized, "Thou hast given a banner to them that fear thee, that it may be displayed because of the truth" (Psalm 60:4).

We must equip our sons and daughters to act with courage and courtesy, valor and virtue, honor and grace. We must teach them to take seriously the opportunity they have now to demonstrate godly manhood and womanhood before their God and King. And this must go from the lofty to the practical: we must train them how to govern their tongues, treat their siblings, and behave themselves honorably in specific circumstances.

In all this, we must communicate the honor it is to serve the King of Kings (Psalm 45:1). We must convey the glory of this calling (Psalm 45:13). We must affirm to our sons and daughters, even as Paul did to his young disciple Timothy, "Let no man despise thy youth; but be thou an example of the believers, in word, in conversation, in charity, in spirit, in faith, in purity" (I Timothy 4:12).

Parents have a great power of influence over the minds and hearts of their children. Their children are almost continually with them—they are seen by them in nearly all they do, in their habitual conduct, and character at home. They are . . . heard in what they say; seen in what they do; studied in all their behavior; by little ears, and eyes, and minds, which are scarcely ever closed!

The child's heart is soft and pliable to a father's or a mother's influence. Their constant influence has been molding him from the dawn of reason. What, then, ought to be the parents' behavior at home? The whole cultivation, and direction, and management of a child's mind, from the very dawn of reason, should be carried on with special reference to the formation of Christian character. This should be the one thing, to which all other things should be in subordination.

The pious parents, who embody a meek, benevolent, ardent, and consistent godliness in their character, exert a tremendous influence over the minds of their children!

—*John Angell James,*
The Christian Professor, *1837*

The apostolic counsel of 'diligence' in ruling throws light upon the nature and aim of authority; it is no longer a matter of personal honour and dignity; authority is for use and service, and the honour that goes with it is only for the better service of those under authority. The arbitrary parent, the exacting parent, who claims this and that of deference and duty because he is a parent, all for his own honour and glory, is more hopelessly in the wrong than the parent who practically abdicates; the majesty of parenthood is hedged round with observances only because it is good for the children to 'faithfully serve, honour, and humbly obey' their natural rulers. Only at home can children be trained in the chivalrous temper of 'proud submission and dignified obedience'; and if the parents do not inspire and foster deference, reverence, and loyalty, how shall these crowning graces of character thrive in a hard and emulous world?

—*Charlotte Mason*, Parents and Children

What we want to do with our children is not merely to control them and keep them in order, but to implant true principles deep in their hearts which shall rule their whole lives; to shape their character from within into Christlike beauty, and to make of them noble men and women, strong for battle and for duty. They are to be trained rather than governed. Growth of character, not merely good behavior, is the object of all home governing and teaching. Therefore the home influence is far more important than the home laws, and the parents' lives are of more moment than their teachings.

—*J.R. Miller*, The Family, 1882

Wherein lies then the maintenance of God's order in the family? The answer to this question is found in both Ephesians and Colossians. (Eph.5: 22-33, Eph.6: 1-9; Col. 3: 18-25, Col. 4: 1.) The husband is the head, and as such has to act as God's vice-regent, to govern not according to his, but according to the divine will. The authority put into his hands is from the Lord, and it is his to wield for Him, and it cannot therefore be delegated to another. The wife is in subjection to her husband, even as the Church is subject to Christ, the husband on his part having to love his wife even as Christ loved the Church, and gave Himself for it. The responsibility of children is to obey their parents in the Lord. Their obedience is to be absolute, qualified only by the condition—in the Lord.

With these instructions before us, it is easy to perceive that if the wife govern instead of the husband, or if the children are permitted to have their own way, to please themselves instead of living in subjection; it could not be productive either of blessing, harmony, or happiness. No; the pathway of blessing is the pathway of obedience in the several spheres we are called upon to fill. And when this is acknowledged by the various members of a family, that household becomes a testimony for God in a scene where all have departed from Him—a bright circle of light in the midst of surrounding darkness.

—*E. Dennett,* God's Order, *1882*

Man covers the face of the earth with his achievements and his triumphs, while woman develops the heart of the world, and leads it in paths of pleasantness and peace. Fatherhood implies kingly strength, conquest, and guidance, while Motherhood wears the royal purple of queen in the domain of the home, the affections, the pure loves, undying hopes and dear memories that inspire and guide our lives.

—*D.H. Wever,* The Mother's Legacy, *1908*

The home is a seminary of infinite importance. It is important because it is universal, and because the education it bestows gives color to the whole texture of life. The things said there give bias to character far more than do sermons, lectures, newspapers, and book. No other teachers have acknowledged the divine right to instruct children that is granted without challenge to parents. The foundation of our national life is in their hands. They can make it send forth waters bitter or sweet, for the death or the healing of the people.

The smallest bit of opinion sown in the minds of children in private life later issue forth to the world and become its public opinions, for nations are gathered out of nurseries.

—*The Golden Gems of Life*

Christian parents, brothers and sisters in Christ, there is no greater calling in our lives as Christians than to raise up the next generation of faithful servants of the Lord Jesus Christ. Surely within that calling, the most noble, the most necessary, the most foundational task is to ensure our children have been thoroughly trained to properly, earnestly, honestly, from the heart and soul and mind and strength, offer their reasonable service, their spiritual worship to God the Father Almighty in the name of His only begotten Son, our Lord and Saviour Jesus Christ through the indwelling power of the Holy Spirit. Amen!

—*Craig and Barbara Smith*

Conclusion

After reading through the inspiring writings contained in this book, my prayer is that you find yourself with renewed vision for what Biblical womanhood is meant to be. Whether you are a daughter, sister, aunt, wife, mother or grandmother, there is a work to be done, and you are needed.

As you begin to grasp just how vitally important your role as the queen of your home is, it is easy to feel a bit overwhelmed. Building a nation, raising an army, training, guiding, guarding, loving, helping and nurturing—as well as changing diapers, washing dishes, wiping cute little noses, doing laundry and tending to a mind-boggling array of other duties around the clock—is a tall order to fulfill. Isn't this all just a bit too much to put on one person? Is it even possible to attain to all these high and lofty ideals? What if we have no idea how to begin?

Take heart! This is where we must remember that we cannot depend on our own strength to do this great work. We are weak, we grow weary, we are sinful, we get tired of laying down our lives for others (we just want to lay down and take a nap), and we can easily lose our vision (it got buried under all those piles of laundry).

When discouragement begins to creep in and you feel like throwing in the towel (or, in this case, the crown), consider just a few of God's many beautiful and sure promises:

My flesh and my heart faileth: but God is the strength of my heart, and my portion for ever. (Psalm 73:26)

It is God that girdeth me with strength, and maketh my way perfect. (Psalm 18:32)

The Lord is my rock, and my fortress, and my deliverer; my God, my strength, in whom I will trust; my buckler, and the horn of my salvation, and my high tower. (Psalm 18:2)

He giveth power to the faint; and to them that have no might he increaseth strength. (Isaiah 40:29)

What does it really mean though to look to Him for strength? How do we find rest when we grow so weary?

What about those days where we feel like we really have given our all, but still have to keep on giving? It sounds wonderful, but how does this actually play out in the day-to-day whirlwind?

I was pondering this myself one day, wondering particularly how "the joy of the Lord is your strength" (Nehemiah 8:10) actually worked. I opened up my Bible to Proverbs 16:20 and found my answer: "Whoso trusteth in the Lord, happy is he."

Our strength comes from our joy in the Lord, and our joy in the Lord comes from our trust in Him.

When we truly trust the Lord, then we rest in Him and no longer rely on our own strength but on Him to hold us up and carry us. Eureka!

It is trust in God and what He says in His Holy Word that keeps our hope and vision alive; without it we lose our purpose and our way. Trust is what causes us to cry out to Him for help and sees Him answer in all the little details. This is where we can find delight and peace and joy like we've never known. This is what we fall back on and what pushes us forward. Our trust in Him strengthens us to obey Him and our obedience leads to even greater trust. It is confidence in Him that undergirds us and gives us a sure foundation on which we can stand even when the winds blow hard. When we are built on the Rock (Matthew 7:24), He holds us up even (and especially) when we come to the end of ourselves.

If we could rise to this high calling in our own strength, we would not learn to depend on the Lord the way we do when we fall exhausted at His feet—and when we learn to depend on Him, then we also glorify Him. Instead of patting ourselves on the back and feeling satisfied with our wonderful accomplishments, we point to our faithful God and know the only reason we accomplish anything is by His grace and mercy.

As daughters of the King of Kings may we rule our little corners of His Kingdom honorably and well. Let us keep our eyes fixed firmly on our Heavenly Father and His Word. Though to the world our heads may look bare, may we earn and wear the crown of glory promised to those who seek wisdom and faithfully persevere:

> *Wisdom is the principal thing; therefore get wisdom: and with all thy getting get understanding. Exalt her, and she shall promote thee: she shall bring thee to honour, when thou dost embrace her. She shall give to thine head an ornament of grace: a crown of glory shall she deliver to thee. (Proverbs 4:7)*

May we never forget the might and power of our calling and our utter dependence on our Heavenly King to fulfill our role as queen of the home.

End Notes

[1] Doug Phillips in "The Daughter of Destiny" *Verses of Virtue*. Published by Vision Forum, 2007.

[2] *Passionate Housewives, Desperate for God* by Stacy McDonald and Jennie Chancey. Preface. Published by Vision Forum, 2007.

About the Author

Jennifer McBride is the blessed wife of Steve and the happy mother of eight children ages ten and under. She loves teaching (and learning with) her

The McBride Family

children, reading, writing, history, sewing and a good cup of tea. In her sparest of spare moments, she maintains NobleWomanhood.com, a website dedicated to proclaiming the nobility and power of Biblical womanhood and reclaiming the lost arts of homemaking.

Notes

Notes

Notes

Notes

Notes

Notes